I0214509

The 7 Secrets to Successful Apartment Leasing

Find Quality Renters, Fill Vacancies, and Maximize Your Rental Income

Eric Cumley

McGraw-Hill

New York Chicago San Francisco Lisbon London
Madrid Mexico City Milan New Delhi San Juan
Seoul Singapore Sydney Toronto

The McGraw-Hill Companies

1 2 3 4 5 6 7 8 9 0 FGR/FGR 0 9 8 7 6 5

ISBN 978-0-07-183170-3

Library of Congress Cataloging-in-Publication Data

Cumley, Eric.
The 7 secrets to successful apartment leasing: find quality renters, fill vacancies, and maximize your rental income/Eric Cumley.
p. cm.
Includes index.

1. Real estate management—United States—Handbooks, manuals, etc. 2. Landlord and tenant—United States—Handbooks, manuals, etc. 3. Rental housing—United States—Handbooks, manuals, etc. I. Title: Seven secrets to successful apartment leasing. II. Title.
HD1394.5.U6C86 2005
333.33'8—dc22 2005022320

This book is dedicated to my parents:

Bill, who taught me to
set the hook and squeeze the trigger;
and
Gwen, who has blanketed me
with a lifetime of earnest prayer

Contents

ACKNOWLEDGMENTS

With special thanks to:

Gene Chamberlain and *Toni Blake*, for educating and motivating me throughout my apartment leasing career. You have raised the standards of excellence in our industry, and are to be greatly commended for the contributions you have made;

Jim Kirkpatrick and *Mick Morris*, my mentors at *For Rent Magazine*, for showing me that the secret to success lies in helping others get what they want. It is an honor and a privilege to have worked with you both;

Don and Linda Crace, Kurt Armbruster, Nan Drake, Jim Eeckhoudt, Saeed Kaley, and *Chuck Stringer*, my esteemed associates with Dale Carnegie Training. Each of you helped me to "earn the right," and for that I am especially grateful;

John Mullally and *Jerry Maxwell* of Mullally Development Company, for believing in me and supporting my ideas from the very beginning;

My ingenious brother *Kevin*, who not surprisingly unlocked what was perhaps the most mystifying secret of all;

Larry Diamond, for your encouragement and excellent, straight-ahead advice;

Sheryn, for telling me the things I needed to hear (even when I didn't particularly want to hear them);

Victoria McCown, Supervising Editor for this project;

And last, but certainly not least, the many apartment industry professionals—assistant managers, housekeepers, leasing consultants, maintenance technicians, owners, property managers, resident managers, and vendors—who have so generously shared their ideas and experiences with me over the years.

I would also like to express my sincere gratitude to the following members of the Institute of Real Estate Management (IREM), Western Washington Chapter #27, who thoughtfully reviewed portions of this book prior to its publication:

Deborah Coombs, CPM
Sloan Jordan, CPM
Patrick Welton, CPM

Diana Dibble, ARM
Catie Friedrich, ARM
Tina Gordon-Phelan, ARM
Nita Kirrage, ARM
Patrick Nichols-McCarty, ARM
Nancy Scott, ARM
Kristin Stacey ARM
Beth Ann Syjud, ARM
Carrise Torres, ARM

The contributions and feedback provided by this distinguished group of experts have greatly enhanced the value of this book as an apartment industry resource.

Thank you all for your time and assistance.

Introduction

> *The loss of focus on the customer as a human being is probably the single most important fact about the state of service and service management in the Western world today.*
>
> Dr. Karl Albrecht, *The Only Thing That Matters*

With all the changes that the apartment industry has seen in the last 20 years, none have been quite so dramatic as the ways in which apartments themselves have changed. Once rather plain and largely undramatic, apartment homes of today have become extraordinary expressions of luxury and convenience. Natural gas fireplaces, kitchens equipped with the latest technologies, attached garages, full-size gymnasiums, racquetball courts, jet lap pools, movie theaters, and built-in alarm systems are less the exception and more the rule now than ever before.

But not only the apartments have changed. In many parts of the country, the sheer *number* of apartments has changed as well. Where pastures and sleepy suburbs once rested, apartment developments now sprawl as far as the eye can see. And although new apartment construction has generally slowed in recent years, the tremendous explosion seen in multifamily development over the last decade created some challenges that remain with us yet today.

Among the toughest of those challenges is found in market areas where apartment supply exceeds demand. High vacancies linger month after month. Companies invest hundreds of thousands of dollars in advertising, marketing, and special promotions to attract qualified residents. With rents in many parts of the country comparable to the monthly mortgage payment on a single-family "starter home" (in the present economic climate), more and more of those qualified residents are moving out of apartments and into houses every day.

What does this mean for the apartment industry? Among other things, it means that competition for qualified apartment renters is growing stiffer all the time, especially in large metropolitan areas with massive inventories of apartments. In short, it means that the rules of the game are changing.

WHY THIS BOOK WAS WRITTEN

During a period spanning from the mid-1980s well into the 1990s, the marketing energies of the apartment industry shifted from the conventional to the spectacular and unrestrained. As increasing numbers of apartments were built and market areas grew soft, the industry began leaning heavily on enormous rent concessions. Lavish vacation giveaways. Extravagant community events. Radio campaigns. Guerrilla direct mail. Billboards. Bus cards. The list went on and on. In fact, it wouldn't be surprising if somebody somewhere even gave skywriting a try, considering how feverish the race for new and clever ideas had become.

In many cases, however, this tremendous shift in emphasis toward marketing resulted in an equal and corresponding shift away from what is arguably the most critical factor in the apartment leasing equation: *human relations skills*. This is not to say that clever marketing campaigns are unimportant; on the contrary, innovative marketing is crucial to reducing and preventing high vacancy. However, marketing is often heralded as *the* solution to high vacancy, when in truth it is not. Marketing is only *a means by which we achieve* the solution to high vacancy. Put another way, all marketing does, as someone once said, is "get the phone to ring and the door to swing." It does not win the trust and loyalty of prospective residents. It does not welcome them warmly on their move-in day. Nor does it go the extra mile for them when eventually they're in need of service. Those jobs always have been—and always will be—the responsibility of leasing office professionals skilled in dealing with people.

This book was written to establish an emphasis on human relations skills as the secret to long-term success in the apartment industry. Some people casually dismiss the study of human relations as an exercise in the elementary, saying "Oh, we've heard it all before. It's just common sense." Funny thing is, for the most part they're right. Many of the secrets to effectively dealing with people and achieving success in apartment leasing are indeed nothing more than common sense approaches to relating with others. But just because something is common sense doesn't necessarily mean that it's common *practice*. In fact, common sense doesn't count for anything unless and until it is applied.

WHO SHOULD READ THIS BOOK?

Anyone who has an interest in whether apartments are vacant or occupied should read this book. While it was written primarily with the challenges of front-line leasing professionals in mind, its relevance extends to anyone involved with the business of leasing apartments, because it is a book about relationship building. Regardless of who you are or the role for which you are responsible, success in the apartment business boils down to the quality of the relationships you build and maintain.

If you are an apartment owner, this book will broaden your perspectives not only about how apartment shoppers respond to what your building has to offer, but also about how they are served once they come into contact with your leasing office staff. Whether you own one apartment or one thousand, you'll be able to positively influence your profits—and enhance the value of your investment—by advocating the techniques you'll read about here.

If you're a property management company executive (president, vice president, property manager/supervisor, director of marketing, etc.) this book is of particular importance. The apartment industry is a mentoring industry; much of a leasing professional's success (or lack thereof) depends upon what that person receives in the way of on-the-job training. This applies not only to rookies, but also to veterans and all experience levels in between. As an executive, you are looked upon by your employees as both a leader and an expert, due largely to the fact that you've risen to the position of influence you now enjoy. Filtering the ideas in this book through your own experiences, you can use them to continually guide and reinforce the leasing techniques used by your team. In the process, you'll emerge a stronger, more effective leader—one who inspires greater confidence and better performance from the people under your supervision.

If you're a leasing office professional (resident manager, assistant manager, or leasing consultant) this book was written especially for you. It is the product not only of my own experiences in apartment leasing and customer relations, but those of numerous other experts in our industry as well (see the Acknowledgments). Within the following pages, you'll discover hundreds of ways to increase your self-confidence and strengthen your ability to earn the business of qualified apartment shoppers. You'll receive inspiration and encouragement to help you when faced with difficult situations. And in what are certain to be a number of cases, you'll be challenged to take a much closer look at how you approach the leasing process.

If you work in maintenance or housekeeping services, this book could be your ticket to a new career path. Many property management professionals—including senior level executives—began their careers by serving in maintenance or housekeeping roles. However, rising from one level to the next requires a solid foundation built upon know-how and desire. This book, combined with direction and encouragement from your coworkers in the leasing office, will provide you with the know-how. You alone must provide the desire. So long as the right combination of know-how and desire is present, there is virtually no limit to the things you can accomplish.

This book is also recommended for professionals who provide support services to the apartment industry (known as *vendors*). Those who specialize in credit screening, furniture rentals, apartment advertising, landscaping, locator services, and so on will all benefit from a broader understanding of apartment leasing mechanics. The more vendors know about the workings of the leasing office and the challenges encountered therein, the better they can tailor their products and services to meet the needs of the industry.

Finally, if you're just now considering a career in apartment management, *The 7 Secrets to Successful Apartment Leasing* is an excellent place to begin. It is the most detailed and practical overview of professional apartment leasing techniques available on the market today. Since leasing is the foundation for success in apartment management, most people enter the "white collar" side of the business as leasing consultants. Gaining front-line experience in the leasing office is without question the best way to acquire the knowledge and skill you'll need as you "climb the ladder of success."

WHAT YOU CAN EXPECT FROM THIS BOOK

It is important for you to know right up front that there are a number of topics this book does not cover in great detail. For example, advertising and marketing, resident retention, and the Fair Housing Act have been left largely unaddressed, for two reasons. First, top priority was placed on revealing the secrets to effective communication between leasing professionals and their future residents. Second, it was essential that the book be kept at a readable size and an affordable price.

It is also important to point out that *The 7 Secrets to Successful Apartment Leasing* is not intended as a book of answers. Rather, it should be looked upon as a resource of *ideas*. It offers practical suggestions supported by detailed examples. It inspires, it motivates, and it challenges. In short, it was born of a desire to provide the apartment industry with people-based solutions for achieving higher occupancy.

In closing, let me say that not every idea in the following pages is likely to fit you like a glove. No two styles are exactly alike; what fits mine may not fit yours, and vice versa. Maybe you're just now starting in the business. Maybe you've been in it for years. Maybe you've got one apartment to lease. Maybe you've got 12. Maybe you've got 1,200—there is no possible way to know. Maybe yours is a conventionally financed community, and maybe it's government subsidized. There are simply far too many variables in the apartment leasing business to accommodate within the pages of a single book. But that's okay. Where my ideas leave off, the ideas of others will pick up. The success building process involves acquiring

different perspectives, and in my opinion the more we can get our hands on the better.

By the way, if you purchased this book under the impression that all you were getting were seven secrets to successful apartment leasing, I have a special message just for you:

Get ready for a *very* pleasant surprise.

Secret Number 1

The Telephone Is Your Lifeline to Leasing Success

You ain't learnin' nothin' when you're doin' all the talkin'.

Sign in the office of Rep. Lyndon B. Johnson,
later to become the 36th president of the United States

Lisa (bored, answering in a monotone): Meadows Apartments.
Caller: Oh, hi. Do you have any two bedrooms?
Lisa: Uh huh. They're $725.00.
Caller: Okay (pausing, unsure what to say next).
Lisa: Wanna come take a look?
Caller: Well, I just started calling around.
Lisa: All right. Our office hours are Monday through Friday, 9 to 6, and weekends, 10 to 5. You can swing by any time.
Caller: Sounds good. Thanks.
Lisa: Uh huh. Buh—bye.

I recently conducted a study with a company that evaluates leasing staff performance across the Northwest. One hundred "shopper evaluation" reports were selected at random, then examined to see how each person had scored on their phone techniques.

The results were shocking. Out of 100 evaluations, *none* were rated excellent. Not one. The number of above average performances was 12—slightly better, but not nearly what was expected. Thirty-three of the people scored average, and a whopping fifty-five came in below average.

In total, *88 percent* of the people evaluated received average ratings or worse.

It took some time before what I had found began to sink in. On the average, 88 percent of the people answering leasing office telephones across the Pacific Northwest weren't doing a very good job of it (and I suspect the nationwide trend may not be much different).

But then a welcome ray of optimism broke through. These statistics suggest that if an apartment leasing professional is not turning in top-caliber performance on the telephone, 88 percent of that person's *competitors are not* either.

All of a sudden, the news didn't look quite so bad.

PREPARATION MAKES THE DIFFERENCE

College basketball coach Bobby Knight once said that "you've got to have more than the will to win. You've got to have the will to *prepare* to win." How right he was. Preparation determines the difference between mediocrity and excellence, and regardless of a person's level of experience, consistent preparation always pays off. The more you prepare, the better you'll be able to communicate about your apartments in ways that will interest callers the most. As your skills increase through preparation, you're more apt to be regarded as experts—people worth listening to.

Preparation in advance of answering the telephone is vitally important; more opportunities to win new residents come to us via the telephone than from all other sources combined. Before you pick up another call in the leasing office, be sure to prepare as thoroughly as possible in the following five areas:

Be ready with the tools of the trade. Disorganization can be costly. Telephone presentations that commence with a frantic search for some-

thing to write on, write with, or read from generally do not begin well. Always be sure to have a pen, guest card, your list of available apartments, current pricing information, and brochures within easy reach. As you'll see secret number 4, you can also assemble a community information notebook to organize leasing materials and make them more accessible on a moment's notice.

Prepare information about your apartments. Your goal should be to acquire more knowledge about our apartments than we'll ever need. In other words, since you never know what questions callers are going to ask, you should build up "reserve power" when it comes to apartment information. The reason is kind of like Murphy's Law: The unlikeliest people seem to ask the toughest questions at the least-expected times.

Rather than being caught unaware, prepare for as many questions as you can by doing some preliminary research. When were your apartments built? What are the insulation, or *R values*, throughout? How are both the interior walls and shared walls constructed? How can your residents maximize the performance of their fireplaces or air conditioners? How does a person read the circuit breaker diagram? What does it take to operate the intercom system? Gather as much information for your apartments as you can—both technical and otherwise—but understand that you won't always cover every detail each time you pick up the phone. In fact, offering too much information over the phone is a big mistake. Generally speaking, you want to present only the information that will interest your callers the most.

It's also important to recognize that you need to do more than merely gather information about the *features* of your apartments. For example, let's say that you offer full-size washers and dryers. Of course, an individual washer and dryer would be nice for a person to have, but *why*? Asking yourself this question about every available feature will help you discover the *benefits* of what those features provide. For example, with in-unit laundry machines residents enjoy optimum convenience and peace of mind. Since benefits are what people ultimately experience in day-to-day living, benefit-oriented information is what future residents are usually most interested to hear. Facts and features, for the most part, are boring by themselves. As you'll see further in the discussion on demonstrations, apartments take on a whole new appeal when they are presented in terms of the lifestyle benefits they can provide.

Therefore, when preparing specific information about your apartments and the benefits they offer, continually ask yourself this question: How does this [particular feature] translate into benefits that people will appreciate and enjoy?

Finally, be ready to describe your various floorplans, carpet colors, view locations, lifestyle amenities, and so forth in vivid detail. This is also information that can be assembled in your Community Information Notebook for quick and easy reference while on the phone.

Prepare information about your community and the surrounding area. A common mistake made on the phone is to assume that people calling an apartment community are familiar with the area. The fact is, few callers are likely to be as familiar with the advantages of your community design and surrounding neighborhood conveniences as you.

You'll want to be thoroughly prepared with information about your apartment community itself, as well as about the particular advantages of living in your area. Take time to write this information down, and keep it near your phone at all times. Depending on the specific interests of your caller, you can refer to your notes until you can speak with confidence about the primary benefits of your community and its location.

Prepare information about your competitors. Before answering the leasing office phone, it is very important that you gather information about the competition in your area. Most prospects calling you are also calling your competitors and may tell you things like "I was just talking with the people over at Cherry Lane, and they offer free covered parking. I don't see covered parking listed in *your* ad." While Cherry Lane may indeed enjoy an edge over you in parking, their apartments might also have less storage space, which could be a more important issue to the caller when pointed out. This is why it is so important to know precisely what your competitors have to offer. Not knowing puts you at a dramatic disadvantage in the marketplace.

When you present information about your competitors over the phone, do so in as objective a manner as possible. Professional ethics must prevail. Moreover, cooperative relationships with competitors can be very

beneficial; if you're on friendly terms, they'll probably send you referrals whenever their occupancy rates are high. Therefore, when talking to callers about your competitors, avoid making critical or disparaging comments at all costs. (Additional ideas for diplomatically referring to competitors appear in Secret 5.)

Prepare for frequently encountered objections. I first experienced the value of preparing for frequently encountered objections while working as the assistant manager on a brand-new "lease up" community. Instead of having been equipped with washers and dryers in each apartment, the property had been designed with community laundry centers. When we learned that our toughest competitors offered either full-size and stack machines or hookups in their apartments, it became apparent that the issue of laundry was going to be a major competitive factor.

At first, many callers—upon learning that our community had laundry centers—would simply insist that they needed a washer and dryer in their apartment and hang up. We quickly realized that until we came up with a way to help people more rapidly appreciate the benefits of community laundry centers, we would continue to lose calls.

The secret, we discovered, was to introduce the laundry issue before our callers raised it themselves: "*Another great advantage to living at Crown Pointe is that the community has been designed with state-of-the-art laundry centers. Laundry centers are an excellent alternative to individual washers and dryers, for a number of reasons.*

"*First, washers and dryers can take up a lot of space in an apartment. Without them, apartments at Crown Pointe offer over 100 cubic feet more living and storage space for your money. Second—and this is very important—laundry machines consume a lot of electricity, which is a hidden energy cost people often don't consider. Finally, what our residents say they like best is that they can do three or four loads of laundry in the time it normally takes to do just one. You save space, you save money, and you save time. It really is a great way to go.*"

Whether it relates to laundry or to something else, when you take an objection you know you're likely to hear and address it before your caller makes it an issue, you can often eliminate it as a threat to the success of your presentation. The key, as you just saw, is to present what you offer in positive, benefit-oriented terms. Simply address the matter (for example, your community may lack exercise facilities), translate that fact into one or two key benefits (your residents get better value for their dollar as well as discounted memberships at a nearby health club), and then present those benefits with enthusiasm. Preparing for frequently encountered objections will enable you to effectively move beyond ones that may have compelled callers to hang up on you in the past.

WHEN YOUR TELEPHONE RINGS

The instant your telephone begins ringing is a crucial moment in the early stages of the leasing process. Before you pick up a call there are five things you can do to ensure that each presentation you make begins strongly:

If serving another customer, excuse yourself. If you have a prospect or a resident in your office when your phone starts to ring, ask that person to excuse you while you pick up the call. When you do, explain to your caller as quickly and politely as possible that you're in the process of serving another customer. Ask for the caller's name and number, write them down, reassure them that you'll return their call as soon as you're able, and then thank them for their patience as you close. Your goal in situations like these is to make both the caller *and* the person in your office feel like top priorities.

Stop whatever you're doing at your desk. Briefly close your eyes and take a deep breath. Take a moment to mentally shift gears, rev up your positive energy, and get focused on the full range of your product knowledge.

Answer on the first or second ring. Much has been said about the issue of how many times a phone should ring before being answered. Some people caution against answering on the first ring, saying that to do so would be overly eager. But let's face it—we live in an information *now* society. The faster our service, and the more time we can save our customers, the better. Besides, the number of rings we hear in our offices doesn't always coincide with the number of rings heard on the other end of the line. The caller might hear two rings by the time we've only heard one. So pick up on the first or second ring. Either is just fine.

However, there is one issue on which most apartment industry experts agree. Avoid letting your phone ring more than three times. It's amazing

how quickly callers grow impatient, hang up, and begin dialing the next number on their list.

Look upward, and smile. Believe it or not, you can hear a smile over the phone. If you doubt it, try this experiment with the answering device either at home or in your office. Record an outgoing message with your head hung low and a scowl on your face. Play it back a few times, and get a clear impression of the result. Then look up, smile, and record the exact same message again. Done sincerely, you'll notice a dramatic positive difference in the second recording over the first. This is the very difference your callers can hear when you look up and smile before answering.

Remember the incredible power of enthusiasm. The word "enthusiasm" is derived from two Greek words—*en*, meaning "in," and *theos*, which is the Greek word for God. The English word *enthusiasm* literally means "God within."

The essence of the word enthusiasm should not be confused with boisterous speech or wild activity. Rather, genuine enthusiasm is a positive, purposeful energy that radiates from the *inside out*. A person's enthusiasm, or lack thereof, is a mirror reflection of their passion for people and life. It is also a measure of a person's excitement about sharing that passion with others. Are you excited about the challenge of leasing apartments? Are you excited about the positive differences you are capable of making in other people's lives? And do you have a passion for helping others get what they want?

If so, then there is no question that you qualify as an enthusiastic person. Always remember the extraordinary, magnetic power of enthusiasm. And remember that the extent to which your caller's interest grows or fades will depend on the enthusiasm they hear in your voice. Projected over the telephone, enthusiasm will catapult your performance to amazing new heights, and leave impressions in the mind of your caller that will not soon be forgotten.

WHEN YOU ANSWER, WHAT SHOULD YOU SAY?

There are an endless number of ways that people answer their phones in the leasing office. See if you can find your style (or one close to it) in the following examples:

"Victorian Apartments."
"Victorian Apartments, Chris speaking."
"Victorian Apartments, this is Chris. How may I help you?"
"Thank you for calling Victorian Apartments, this is Chris."
"Good morning/afternoon, Victorian Apartments."
"It's a great day at Victorian Apartments, this is Chris."
"Victorian Apartments, may I help you?"

The list could go on and on. Most of the approaches listed here help get conversations off to a good start. However, there are a couple that may be best to avoid.

The first questionable approach is the one that incorporates the phrases "*Good morning*" or "*Good afternoon.*" Of course, these greetings are meant to convey goodwill, and in that sense they're fine. The problem occurs when we answer by saying, "Good morning, Victorian Apartments" at 2:45 in the afternoon. A minor error? Perhaps. But with the marketplace as competitive as it is today, we must strive for *zero error* performance. If we don't, we risk getting blown away by competitors who do.

The second approach is the one that includes the words "*may I help you?*" Ever since we were kids, salespeople have been approaching us with those four little words. Let's say that you've just walked into a clothing store. You haven't been there 30 seconds when all of a sudden, out of the corner of your eye, you see someone swooping in for the kill. It's a *salesperson,* and the first words out of his or her mouth are "May I help you?"

How are you most likely to respond? If you're like most people, you'll probably say "*No thanks. I'm just looking,*" which loosely translated means "Back off and get out of my face." Asking "May I help you" automatically activates the salesperson defense mechanism we all acquire over years of encounters with pushy salespeople. If you've been using *may I help you* in your telephone greetings, consider changing it slightly to "*How may I help you?*" Adding the word *how* invites a caller to explain their individual circumstances, and helps get the call off to a better start.

When it comes to how you answer, you should avoid using language that places your caller's attitude toward you at risk. That is why a friendly, professional greeting is the best way to start your phone conversations.

Here's an example: *"Thank you for calling Victorian Apartments, this is Chris."* The most important points to remember about your greeting is that it be courteous, that it clearly state your community's name, and that it introduces you by name, which gives callers the opportunity to respond with their own names in reply.

PLACING CALLERS ON HOLD

Due to circumstances beyond our control, there are times when we must immediately place calls on hold. However, care must be exercised in how this is done. The longer callers are made to wait, the more impatient and resentful they are likely to become.

Following is an effective plan for placing callers on hold:

- When talking on line one and line two rings in, ask the caller on line one if they will ***please hold for a moment.*** Don't ask them to hold for a second, or a minute; some people will take you literally. A moment, on the other hand, is an indefinable amount of time. It buys you some breathing room in case you can't get right back to the caller you've placed on hold.
- Just before you place caller one on hold, tell them that you'll return to their call as soon as you can. Sometimes even the simplest word of reassurance will prevent them from hanging up in frustration if your time with the second caller runs longer than expected.
- Place caller one on hold, and answer the call on line two. As soon as you possibly can, explain that you are serving a customer on another line and that you'll have to return their call. Ask for your second caller's full name, as well as for a number where they can be reached. Make sure this information gets written down where it won't be lost or forgotten.
- Return to caller one. Instead of apologizing for the delay with a comment like "Sorry about that," ***thank them for waiting.*** Why say you're sorry? And what is there to be sorry about? Whenever possible, replace negative language with positive alternatives.
- Finally, once you've finished with caller one, keep your promise to caller two and return their call at your soonest opportunity.

Efficiently managing multiple calls takes practice, but putting forth the extra effort is worth it. Try incorporating these ideas when you are faced with placing callers on hold. You'll increase your odds of having not just one, but *two* prospects who are interested in learning more about the apartments you have to offer.

BUILDING THE CONVERSATION

Before making a telephone presentation, you must first have an objective. What do you want to accomplish with the call? The main objective of a leasing telephone presentation is *to gain a commitment from the caller that will move them to the next stage in the leasing process*.

The next stage, of course, is an appointment to meet in person. Building an effective telephone conversation that will increase your chances of actually meeting the caller involves the following five steps:

1. Asking the Right Questions
2. Establishing Your Caller's Qualifications
3. Being a First-Rate Listener
4. Describing Apartments to Your Callers
5. Scheduling an Appointment to Meet

Let's begin by examining the types of questions that can best help turn phone calls into face-to-face meetings.

Asking the Right Questions

For a moment, imagine that you're a professional apartment shopper evaluating the following phone conversation between a leasing consultant and her caller:

Lisa (with enthusiasm): Thank you for calling Evergreen Village, this is Lisa.
Caller: Oh hi. I'm calling about your two bedrooms.
Lisa: Great! Our two bedrooms are about 900 square feet, so they're really spacious. All of our apartments come with washers and dry-
Caller (cutting in): Full size?
Lisa: Uh huh. We have brick woodburning fireplaces, covered park-

ing, forced air electric heat, a tennis court, playground for the kids, built-in microwaves, cathedral ceilings, extra storage . . . let's see, what else. Oh yeah—I almost forgot. We've got an incredible clubhouse with stairclimbers, weight equipment, outdoor pool, sauna, and a big hot tub. We let our residents reserve it for parties and wedding receptions, you know—stuff like that. We're only five minutes from Interstate 1, but it's still really peaceful around here. Let's see, what else do we—

Caller (cutting in again): Do you allow pets?
Lisa (a bit testier this time): Yep. Fifteen pound limit, and there's a $200 fee.
Caller: All right. Well, I just started looking. How much are they?
Lisa: They start at $525.
Caller: Okay. Well, I've got a few more places to call.
Lisa (not swerving from her routine): Sure. Our office hours are Monday through Friday, 9 to 6, and weekends, 10 to 5. Just stop by any time.
Caller: Sounds good. Thanks.
Lisa: You're welcome. Have a nice day. Bye.

As a professional shopper, you would immediately notice two things about this conversation. First, it is a prime example of how 88 percent of phone presentations in our business come off: average, at best. Second, the caller was never encouraged to participate in the exchange. The conversation was almost entirely one way—Lisa's way, that is.

Great telephone presentations usually don't develop when callers are overwhelmed with an avalanche of unsolicited information. Rather, the secret to great phone presentations lies first in learning what's most important to the caller, then tailoring the information to match the preferences they've expressed.

This is done, of course, by asking questions. However, you must carefully consider the nature of the questions you ask. Simply put, your goal should be to ask questions that *get callers talking about themselves.* Unless you get callers talking about themselves, it is impossible to learn

what's most important to them. And unless you learn what is most important to the caller, you simply cannot do an effective job of matching them with a specific apartment. Remember the words of Lyndon Johnson: *You ain't learnin' nothin' when you're doin' all the talkin.'*

Traditional telephone questions. There are a number of traditional approaches to questioning that simply are not well-suited to building early momentum on the phone. Let's start by looking at the type of questions you *don't* want to ask up front.

In the beginning stages of your conversation, it is generally best to refrain from asking questions to which your caller can reply with a basic "yes" or "no." The reason is that yes and no responses tell you almost nothing about the caller. They don't help to reveal the deeper and more important issues in your caller's mind. For example, if you ask a caller, "Are you new to our area?" all they have to do is say yes or no. Neither response will tell you much of anything about them unless they choose to elaborate—which often they do not.

Next, let's look at a different set of questions many of us have been trained to ask. For years, they've been referred to as the *open-ended questions*, or the "Six W's" **W**ho, **W**hat, **W**here, **W**hen, **W**hy, and ho**W**. Examples of these traditional open-ended questions include, "Who will this apartment be for?" "What is your price range?" "Where are you living now?" "When do you need to move?" And "How did you hear about us?"

The reason these particular questions are better, we've been told, is that they cannot be sensibly answered with a yes or no response—which is true. However, while they do generate responses other than yes and no, the answers they produce are typically rather short. Because the Six W's frequently produce short answers, people asking them quickly find themselves having to ask another question. Pretty soon, the exchange becomes less like a presentation and more like an interrogation. Even worse, when all Six W's have been used, the conversation can stall. This is not to say that these traditional open-ended questions are entirely without value. The point is that they are not the best approach to starting conversations from scratch. What's more, they're the same old questions everybody asks.

That's why I've developed one of the most powerful leasing secrets you may ever discover. It is a questioning technique featuring what I call the *Magic Questions*.

The Magic Questions. The Magic Questions are more effective for building first-time conversations than the traditional open-ended questions, for three reasons:

1. Instead of six questions, there are only two, which makes them easier to remember as you begin a conversation with a total stranger.
2. Once they are asked, there is almost no other probable outcome than for people to start—and in most cases, continue—talking about themselves.
3. They produce an abundance of useful information about your prospect, much of which you never specifically have to ask for.

Here they are—The Magic Questions:

- *Please describe for me . . .*
- *Please tell me about . . .*

You'll notice that, in their elemental form, they are not worded as questions. This is one of the strongest advantages of the Magic Question approach. Each phrase can be easily shaped into questions that fit virtually any style and situation where you need to build a productive conversation.

The Magic Questions are a huge improvement over the open-ended questioning techniques of the past. However, there is one particular instance where even the Magic Questions need some help. That is when the caller asks for the price up front.

Responding to the request for price. One of the most difficult challenges faced by leasing professionals on the phone comes when the first two words out of a caller's mouth are "How much?"

For years, many of us have been taught that the best way to respond to requests for price is to immediately answer the question with a question. The idea has been promoted in theory for years, but in live selling situations it can backfire. Here's what often happens: Right off the bat a caller will ask, "How much are your two bedrooms?" Following years of tradition, many leasing consultants respond with a question in reply, like, "How soon do you need one?" And here is where the problem occurs:

In situations like this, the leasing consultant has evaded the caller's question.

Fortunately, there is a better and easier way. When you answer the phone and the first question out of your caller's mouth is, "How much are your two bedrooms?" try responding with an approach like this:

"You know, it really depends on what you're looking for. Would it be okay if we started with just a couple of quick questions?"

There are two powerful customer relations principles at work in this technique:

1. It subtly emphasizes that you cannot realistically quote a price without first understanding the nature of your caller's needs and preferences.
2. Instead of evading the caller's question, it allows you to demonstrate integrity and respect by asking their permission to move the conversation in a slightly different direction. (Actually what you're trying to do is diplomatically create an opportunity to ask a Magic Question and get them talking about themselves.)

Fitting it all together. Let's take a look at how these new ideas—responding to the request for price, and the Magic Questions—might fit together in a real-life telephone scenario:

Lisa (with energy, enthusiasm): Thank you for calling Evergreen Village, this is Lisa.
Caller: How much are your one bedrooms?
Lisa: You know, it really depends on what you're looking for. Would it be okay if we started with just a couple of quick questions?
Caller (a bit impatient): I guess...
Lisa: Great, thanks. First of all, what's your name?
Caller: Bill.
Lisa: Hi, Bill. Again, I'm Lisa. Bill, what's your last name? (proceeds to write Bill's first and last name on a guest card) All right—you said you're looking for a one bedroom. **Could you *please describe for me* some of the things you'd like to have in your new apartment? (Magic Question #1)**

Bill: Well, let's see . . . I need a *big* bedroom. About two years ago when I started living by myself I bought a king-size bed (stops talking at this point)

Lisa: Okay, you need room enough for a king-size bed (writes that down) Got it. What else?

Bill: Another thing I want is a fireplace. I really like to unwind in front of a fire when I come home from work.

Lisa: Sounds great. (writes some more) What else?

Bill: Let me see . . . well, I'd also like to have covered parking. It's something I wish I had where I'm living now.

Lisa: Where is that?

Bill: The Pines, up on SE Thirty-sixth Street.

Lisa: I know right where it is. You were saying about covered parking.

Bill: Yeah . . . I just bought a new truck, and I want to keep it out of the weather, you know?

Lisa: Absolutely. (makes more notes) Okay Bill, let me make sure I've got all this straight. You're looking for a one bedroom—a big one bedroom—with a fireplace and covered parking. What else can you think of?

Bill: Oh, I almost forgot. Two more things, actually. First, I need a good amount of storage. I've got my skis, a mountain bike, golf clubs, and a bunch of other stuff. And second, a washer and dryer would be nice.

Lisa: All right . . . so far so good. (writes more notes) **Next question: Could you *take just a minute and tell me about* where you're living now, and why you've decided to move? (Magic Question #2)**

Bill: Oh boy—are you sure you want me to go into this?

Lisa: I'm sure. It will give me a better sense of the things that are most important to you.

Bill: Okay . . . see, there are these people who live downstairs from me, and they . . . (Bill proceeds to tell Lisa about his experience at The Pines, explaining why he wants to move and how soon. Lisa adds more to her notes.

Lisa: Wow. I'm sorry you had to put up with all of that. You know Bill, it looks like I might be able to help you out.

Bill: Good.

Lisa: How much are you planning to spend?

Bill: Up to about $600, I guess.

Lisa: Great. We definitely fit your budget. Do you have any pets?

Bill: No.

Lisa: Okay. Just a couple more questions, and then I promise I'll stop.

Bill (enjoying the attention): No problem, no problem.

Lisa: How did you find out about us?

Bill: I'm looking at your ad in this magazine I got at the store. It's called the . . . what does this say . . . *Rental Magazine*.

Lisa: Good. Make sure you circle that ad. Now, last question: Can you come out and see me today? I've got an apartment here that you definitely ought to check out.

Bill: Sounds like a good idea. Let's set it up.

The very first thing Lisa did was respond to Bill's request for price using the technique presented earlier: ***You know, it really depends on what you're looking for. Would it be okay if we started with just a couple of quick questions?*** It is, however, important to recognize that not all callers may be as responsive to this approach as Bill. Some simply will not allow further dialogue until you've given them a price. So what should you do if someone insists on the price? *Give it to them*. Just remember that if you are compelled to quote a price, follow it up as immediately as you can with one or two important benefits that add value to your price, like covered parking, cable TV service, free passes to a nearby health club, or whatever. Better yet, ask a question that will encourage your caller to remain on the line. If the caller is willing to cooperate, find out their name and keep things moving. If the caller hangs up, which they sometimes will, at least you'll know that you gave it your best shot.

The beauty of asking the Magic Questions is that they produce a tremendous amount of information about your caller that you don't specifically have to ask for. That's why the Magic Questioning approach feels more like a friendly conversation than it does a sales presentation. As you saw with Lisa, it is common that you'll have to fill in a few details as

you go, using yes/no questions or the Six W's. But most of the time, when asked the Magic Questions, your caller will *volunteer* much of what you need to know.

Now, back to the demonstration. After Lisa temporarily postponed the price issue and learned Bill's name, she asked the first Magic Question: **Could you *please describe for me* some of the things you'd like to have in a new apartment?** As expected, it produced a wide range of valuable information about Bill:

- He lives by himself, so the apartment will be for Bill alone.
- He wants a large bedroom, a fireplace, ample storage, and a washer/dryer in his apartment, as well as covered parking.

Next, Lisa asked Bill the second Magic Question: "**Could you *please tell me about* where you're living now, and why you've decided to move?"** By having him relate his experience at The Pines, Lisa was able to get a better feel for the emotions driving Bill's decision-making process. These emotions, or what are often referred to as "hot buttons," will be very valuable in helping Lisa plan her presentation. Then Bill volunteered one last important item: when he was planning to move.

Finally, Lisa filled in a few remaining gaps: Bill's price range, if he had a pet, and how he found out about Evergreen Village. Using the Magic Questions, combined with genuine interest and enthusiasm, she created a comfortable conversation that produced an abundance of valuable information. But Lisa is not finished yet. There is still more information she needs. In addition, there is the matter of actually getting Bill out to see the apartment. These final steps in the telephone presentation process will be demonstrated near the end of this chapter.

Establishing Your Caller's Qualifications

Even though it wasn't a typical question/answer process, you'll notice that a thorough "qualifying" process took place in Lisa and Bill's conversation. Since your time in the leasing office is very valuable, you want to make certain that callers meet your leasing criteria before you commit to spending more time with them. You don't want to squander precious time with people who are not likely to lease from you. Therefore, it's extremely

important to establish your caller's qualifications, based on the following general guidelines:

The size/type of apartment sought. If you don't have availability in the floorplan a caller needs, or a floorplan that could be a suitable alternative (e.g., substituting a small three bedroom for a two bedroom/two bath), do one of four things. First, add the caller to an active waiting list, and contact them as soon as you know that an apartment of the type they want is coming available. Next, if you work for a company that manages two or more communities, refer them to a "sister community" managed by your company. If you don't have a sister community in the vicinity, consider referring people you can't accommodate to reputable competitors who can. However, before recommending other properties make sure you inspect them first to verify their standards of quality and service. Regardless of whether or not you have an apartment to lease, remember that your main responsibility is to *help that caller*. Placing them on waiting lists first, then referring them to sister communities or competitors (if necessary) promotes long-term cooperation and benefits everyone involved. Lastly, if you can't personally be of service to a prospect, refer them to a reliable apartment locator service if there is one in your area.

The caller's desired move-in date. Your caller's timeframe can be a major influencing factor in how you proceed with the call. There may be times when the caller has an immediate need for a floorplan in which you have nothing available to show. Other callers may be planning their moves weeks or months in advance, making it difficult to know whether or not you'll be able to accommodate them once they're ready to move. Whatever the case, determining your caller's desired move-in date is essential. Without this information it is difficult to effectively manage your time and resources, much less accommodate your caller's needs.

Number of occupants. At the time of this writing, occupancy policies are typically established by apartment owners or companies acting as agents for the owners. Some follow guidelines based on number of occupants allowed per bedroom; others use guidelines based on square footage per person. Whatever the case, you'll need to determine how

many people besides your caller, if any, will be occupying the apartment. A good way to do this is to ask, "Will this apartment just be for yourself, or . . ."? Left open-ended, the caller will usually fill in the blank with the answer you need. The point to remember is that occupancy standards may not be unreasonably restrictive. For the most current guidance on occupancy standards, contact the U.S. Department of Housing and Urban Development (HUD) office nearest you.

Does the caller have pets? if so, what kind and how big? This question is vitally important. If your community accepts pets, and your caller has one, a thorough exchange of information needs to take place. They will need to describe their pet(s), and you will have to fully explain your pet-related policies and requirements. However, many communities don't allow pets, dogs or cats in particular. If yours does not, it doesn't make sense to spend 15 minutes talking with a caller only to discover that she owns a Saint Bernard. If you work at a "no pet" community, address the pet issue early in your presentation. You'll save time and avoid frustration for both yourself and pet owners who call.

The caller's income. When the opportunity presents itself, clearly explain your community income requirements. One common guideline is to require that an applicant's gross monthly income be equal to three or four times the monthly rent. Do the best you can to determine your caller's financial qualifications, without giving offense or arousing irritation. For example, if your community uses the "three times" guideline, you might say, "We ask that all people applying to lease apartments with us have a gross monthly income equal to three times the monthly rent. Does that work for you?" Provided you've already disclosed the rental amount on the floorplan type you've been discussing, the caller can do the math, and in most cases will quickly let you know financially where they stand.

Developing your ability to ask questions may be one of the most valuable customer relations skills you ever learn. Like anything, getting better at gathering valuable information about your callers requires patience, determination, and above all, practice. However, if you make a point of using the Magic Questions in your telephone presentations, you are certain to convert more telephone inquiries into face-to-face opportunities.

Being a First-Rate Listener

After asking the right questions and determining your caller's qualifications, the third step in building great phone presentations is developing the ability to listen. Comedian Jay Leno recently experienced the lighter side of what happens when people fail to listen:

> *"I went into McDonald's yesterday and said, 'I'd like some fries.' The girl at the counter said, 'Would you like fries with that?'"*

Before we think about talking, we need to think about listening. Even though as salespeople we may experience the urge to "make our pitch," we must first be patient—and *listen*. When we talk, we don't learn anything about our caller. And until we learn about our caller, we can't legitimately recommend an apartment to them.

Most experts in the field of apartment leasing are not only exceptional questioners. They are also exceptional listeners. Strategic questioning first gives your prospects the opportunity to talk, which in turn gives you the opportunity to listen and demonstrate your interest in them and their circumstances. Knowing the secrets of when and how to listen is vital in our business of building long-term customer relationships. By using the following techniques, you'll become a better listener—and a stronger leasing professional.

Discipline your inner voice. When we start thinking up responses to what a person is saying before they've finished, we stop listening. Think of how frustrating it is to talk with someone who continually cuts in with "what they think," or how "the same thing happened to them." People like this aren't listening to you; they are simply rehearsing what they're going to say next. For professional salespeople, disciplining the inner voice is one of the most important and most difficult listening skills to master. You must not listen to your prospects with the intent to *reply*. You must instead listen with the intent to *understand.*

Concentrate. Pay close attention to what your caller is saying. Try to ignore and filter out distractions, like paperwork on your desk or things

that are happening outside. Close your eyes periodically and visualize your caller. Better yet, visualize them in the apartment you want them to see. Jealously guard your focus; do not let it be lost.

Try not to interrupt. No matter how relevant the comment may be, interruptions almost always offend those who are interrupted. Each of us knows how irritating it is to be constantly interrupted by know-it-alls. Nevertheless, whether talking on the telephone or face-to-face, we sometimes interrupt by mistake. If you inadvertently interrupt someone, *follow your interruption with another question* as quickly as possible and let the other person continue talking. People are much more likely to forgive an interruption when we return them to the center of the conversation. In addition, the interruption-turned-question will help resume the flow of important information from your caller.

Clarify what you've been told, and repeat it. If you don't completely understand what your caller has said, ask them to explain. It's okay to reveal your need for better understanding; in fact, most people are impressed by that. And like Lisa, periodically repeat the things your prospect says so that they know you understand. When we ask for clarification from our callers in a spirit of genuine interest, and repeat back what's been said, we send clear signals that we're actively listening to every word.

Take notes. You also noticed that Lisa wrote the information she gathered from Bill on a guest card. The importance of taking notes during a telephone presentation cannot be overstated. For one, you can use your notes to refresh your memory and prepare on the day your callers eventually arrive in person. When in person you greet them by name and refer to details they shared over the phone, you create an unforgettable first impression. You can also go right back to the point in the conversation where you last left off (nothing is so frustrating for apartment shoppers than when they provide an abundance of information over the phone, only to be asked for it again in person). Finally, notes can serve as important documentation in the event a grievance involving a caller, other prospect, or resident is filed. For more valuable insights on using guest cards, see pages 54 to 57.

Be an active listener. Be careful not to listen in silence. You may be thought of as distracted or unconcerned. Reassure your caller that you're listening to every word using conversational and relevant phrases like *I see; Go on; Tell me more about [whatever]; Absolutely; That's amazing!; What happened next?; Really?; What else?*; and so forth. Be involved with your callers, and it will be obvious that you care about what's being said.

Here's another secret for people wanting to improve their listening skills: *Never talk more than 30 seconds without giving the other person an opportunity to join in.* Encourage your callers to do much of the talking. When they do, reward them with your undivided and active attention. Ask the right questions, and listen with evident interest. Do this and you will build important bridges of trust and respect in the early stages of your customer relationships.

Describing Apartments to Your Callers

The following may come as a bit of a shock to some, but there really is no other way to break the news. If I'm a renter calling you for information, I don't care about you. I care about *me*. I want to talk in terms of me. Period. *Anything you say that doesn't include me is boring.*

The owner of a local shopping service recently told me that one of the most glaring areas of weakness for leasing professionals on the phone is describing apartments. Your goal in describing apartments must be to paint as vivid and benefit-oriented a picture as you possibly can. More importantly, you need to *put the caller in the picture.*

Lisa gave us an example of the "shotgun" approach so often used when describing apartments over the phone. A long list of apartment features is memorized, then recited in hopes that something will be relevant to the caller. Well, it's not enough that *something* be relevant. *Everything* needs to be relevant. This is where the Magic Questions can make such a dramatic difference in the quality of a phone presentation. *The only way to make truly effective telephone presentations is to learn about the caller's preferences and circumstances first. Then, and only then, can you select and present information about your apartments that is likely to interest your caller.*

Let's say your caller's main preferences are a woodburning fireplace and a large amount of storage space. Assuming that these are features you offer, your challenge is to describe them in such a dramatic and vivid way that your caller can almost feel the heat of a crackling fire on a blustery afternoon. You want them to feel the relief of getting their skis, mountain bikes, and snow tires safely out of the way. Sure, you could simply state that you offer woodburning fireplaces and extra storage. It might even work. But that isn't selling. It's *telling*, and telling almost always excludes the caller.

Therefore, make it your highest priority to put callers at the heart of every "word picture" you paint. Let the competition keep boring *their* callers with memorized lists of irrelevant features. Vividly describe apartments in terms of what's important to your caller, and they'll be far more likely to remember you when the time comes to make their decision.

Scheduling an Appointment to Meet

Think of all the effort you've invested in your telephone presentation up to this point. You've established a friendly rapport with your caller, and you've asked them some intelligent, thought-provoking questions. They've shared important information about themselves, and you've gone the extra mile to paint an appealing picture in their mind's eye of how great it will be coming home to the apartment you've described.

Are you going to throw all this effort away, by telling your callers that they can "swing by any time"? Or are you going to increase the potential for return on your investment by inviting the caller out for a closer look?

Asking qualified callers to come and see an apartment you've described is absolutely essential to maintaining high occupancy. *It is not enough* to recite leasing office hours and tell callers they can just "stop by." Once you've determined that your caller is a prospect with good potential, it is your professional obligation to schedule an appointment.

Let's return to Lisa and Bill. In the closing moments of their conversation, Lisa will demonstrate a variety of effective strategies for getting callers off the phone, into their cars, and out to see an apartment.

Lisa: . . . this is a *great* apartment, and I think it could be a perfect fit. I'll have it all ready and waiting for you when you get here.

Bill: Sounds good. Let's set it up.

Lisa: Will you be making the decision yourself, or will you be making it along with someone else?

Bill: It will just be me.

Lisa: Can you come out and see me today?

Bill (apologetic): Sorry, not a chance. I'm booked solid.

Lisa: Okay, no problem. Let me ask you this: **Is early in the week good for you, or would later in the week be better?**

Bill: Weekends are usually best.

Lisa: Fine. What do you think—**Saturday or Sunday?**

Bill: Let me see . . . I have a softball game at 11:00 on Saturday, and then I'm going to a barbecue on Saturday night. It's looking like Sunday would be better.

Lisa: Morning or afternoon?

Bill: Well, I'll be in church on Sunday morning. It'll have to be afternoon.

Lisa: Great. **Should we make it earlier, say at 1:15? Or later, like 3:45?**

Bill: How about 3:30?

Lisa: Let me check. . . . Okay, that looks good. I'm going to set aside a half an hour so I can give you my undivided attention. **Give me just a moment while I write this down: Sunday, at 3:30 p.m.** (she writes).

Lisa: Bill, **just in case something comes up and we happen to miss each other, let me get a number where you can be reached.** (Bill gives her the number. Lisa repeats it back to confirm.)

Lisa: Do you know how to get here?

Bill (somewhat hesitant): I think so. I'm looking at the map and driving directions in your ad.

Lisa: Let's review the directions real quick, in case you have a question. (They review. Lisa determines where Bill will be starting from, and then provides accurate driving instructions from his location to the community.)

Lisa: Why don't I call you on Saturday to confirm?

Bill: That would be a big help.

Lisa (schedules the call to confirm for Saturday): **If something should happen to come up**, don't worry, just **give me a call** and let me

know. And let me make one more suggestion: **Be sure to bring your checkbook.** If you find the apartment you want—and I think there's a good chance that you will—we'll want to make sure we can get your name on it.

Bill: Sounds good. I'll do that.

Lisa: All right, Bill. I'm looking forward to meeting you. See you Sunday at 3:30 p.m.

Bill: Okay, Lisa. Bye.

Lisa: Bye. **(waits for Bill to hang up first)**

Bill (coming back on the line, urgent): Lisa! Are you still there?

Lisa: I'm right here.

Bill: Oh good! I just remembered a question I've been wanting to ask. How are your apartments heated?

Lisa: The apartment I have in mind for you has electric baseboard heaters in every room. Not only is the system excellent for maintaining a steady temperature, but each room has its own climate control. That way, you can save money by heating only the rooms you want.

Bill: That makes sense. I was just wondering.

Lisa (laughs): Well, I'm glad you caught me. If you have any other questions in the meantime, just give me a call.

Bill: Okay. Gotta go. See ya.

Lisa: Take care, Bill. Bye.

Let's examine these appointment setting strategies, one by one:

Will you be making the decision yourself, or will you be making it along with someone else? Lisa leads off with this question to neutralize a common deflection known as "third party approval." If someone else besides the caller must also be involved in making the decision, it's best to get all the necessary players out to see the apartment at the same time. Otherwise, the chances of gaining a commitment on the caller's first visit are diminished. They'll have to bring someone else back for another look, which can increase the risk of losing them to a competitor.

Can you come out and see me today? Two important principles are at work in this question. Number one, Lisa isn't asking Bill to come see an apartment; she's asking him to come see *her*. This does much more to strengthen the caller's level of personal obligation. Number two, she asked if he could see the apartment *today*. When a caller's level of interest and excitement is high, invite them out to see the apartment on the same day of their call. The more time goes by, the more people's enthusiasm tends to fade.

At this point in the conversation, Lisa begins using a method for setting appointments known as the *funnel technique* (created by the legendary Gene Chamberlain, perhaps the greatest authority on leasing our industry has ever known). The key to its effectiveness lies in the way it guides the caller through a series of pressure-free, easy to make decisions. The options move from broad to specific, thus "funneling" the caller into a day and time that fits best alongside other commitments in their schedule:

Is early in the week usually best, or would later in the week be better? The process starts with a broad look at the caller's entire week.

Saturday or Sunday? Now the caller has to think of two days in particular. They still have the benefit of choosing which is most convenient, but we're gently guiding their decision along.

Morning or afternoon? After Bill chooses Sunday, the process naturally continues and causes him to narrow his decision down even further.

Should we make it earlier, say around 1:15? Or later, like around 3:45? Now Bill has to make a real commitment. The reason is that he has more or less eliminated any excuses not to. Notice also that Lisa uses times on the quarter-hour. This technique subtly conveys that you manage your time carefully, and that it is not to be taken lightly.

After committing Bill to a specific date and time using the funnel technique, Lisa continues building a stronger level of commitment using a variety of effective methods:

Give me just a minute while I write this down. When callers know that their name is written in your appointment book, they tend to feel more obligated. They're "on paper."

Just in case . . . let me get a number where you can be reached. Always make sure you ask for your caller's telephone number, and repeat it to make sure you have it correctly. Try to get numbers for both

work and home if possible, and remember this: If a caller refuses to give you their phone numbers, one of two things could be happening. First, the caller could be hiding something, in which case they may not be someone with whom you want to do business anyway. Second, the caller could be security-conscious. If this is the impression you get, let them know that you respect their privacy, and then politely proceed with the rest of the presentation.

Let's review the directions. Just because someone is looking at a map or printed driving directions in an ad does not necessarily mean they can find their way. The last thing you want is for your prospects to get lost en route to your community, or to pull into a competitor's property by mistake. That's why it is a good idea to review directions before hanging up. And if possible, direct your callers along a route that bypasses your main competitors as an additional strategy for increasing your odds.

Why don't I call you on Saturday to confirm? A call to confirm serves as an effective and considerate reminder to your prospect. Many things can happen in the lives of our callers between the time they call and the time of their visit. In fact, in the meantime they may forget about their appointment altogether. Help make it easier for them to keep their end of the bargain. And if you tell your caller you will call to confirm, you MUST remember to make the call. Schedule it where you won't forget. Make certain that it goes through, on time.

If something should happen to come up . . . give me a call. Your time is valuable, and you want it put to good use. However, waiting around for "no shows" can be a waste. Plant a seed of responsibility in your caller's mind by encouraging them to notify you in case they have to cancel. You're entitled to the courtesy.

Be sure to bring your checkbook. One of the most frustrating moments we encounter is when the prospect is prepared to put down a deposit—but doesn't have the means to pay. They then have to leave the property, which means you may never see them again. Your objective is to arrange the appointment in such a way that you have the best chance of taking a deposit on the caller's first visit. In a tactful and positive way, encourage people to come prepared with the means to reserve an apartment. Putting down a deposit is the *only way* a prospect can guarantee that they'll get the apartment they want.

Waits for Bill to hang up first. Lisa had the presence of mind to keep listening, and it paid off with yet another opportunity to continue earning Bill's loyalty. Start waiting for your callers to hang up first. It won't be long before this practice pays off for you, too.

ONE LAST TELEPHONE TIP

Let's say that you've just completed a top-caliber telephone presentation, and your caller scheduled an appointment to see an apartment. However, the day they want to come out just happens to be your day off.

Provided you have the staff, your best bet in situations like this is to have an associate meet with the caller in your absence. Inform the caller that you will not be in the office on the day they come in, and reassure them that they will receive exceptional service from the person who will be covering in your place. Then, remember this last little tip: Instead of making the call to confirm as you normally would, *instruct your co-worker to make it instead.* Doing this helps to establish a degree of familiarity between your co-worker and your prospect before the visit, and increases the probability that a favorable connection will be made in your absence.

REVIEW

In this secret, we discussed a wide assortment of secrets and techniques that, when consciously applied, can raise your telephone presentation skills to extraordinary new levels:

- Prepare, prepare, prepare! Before making a telephone presentation, make sure you have all the tools you'll need. Obtain as much information about the different aspects of your apartments, your community, the neighborhood, and your competition as possible. In addition, prepare for objections you know are likely to come up. *There's no better way to instill confidence in your caller than to be completely familiar with your apartments and at ease with your knowledge of them.*

- The manner in which you answer your telephone has a significant impact on how callers ultimately perceive you and the community you represent.
- To build a great conversation, ask the Magic Questions. Then, make sure you establish your caller's qualifications in relation to the size/type of apartment they want, their desired move-in date, the number of intended occupants, whether or not they have pets, and their gross monthly income.
- Become a first-rate listener by disciplining your inner voice, concentrating on your caller, and trying not to interrupt. It also helps to clarify what's been said, take notes, and be an active listener.
- Describe your apartments with the caller at the forefront of your mind. Everything you say should be relevant to your caller. Build vivid "word pictures" that include them at every turn.
- Study the secrets to scheduling appointments, and use them in varying combinations to increase the number of callers who actually show up in person. By getting more prospects off the phone and into your office, your overall number of leases will dramatically increase.
- If your caller can only come out on your day off, inform them that your co-worker will assist them instead. Then, to facilitate the "hand off," instruct your co-worker to call the prospect before their actual visit.
- Finally, remember that the telephone is your lifeline to higher occupancy. Make the most of every opportunity it brings to you each day.

Secret Number 2

Warm and Friendly Greetings Build the Foundation for Success

A bit of fragrance always clings to the hand that gives roses.

Chinese proverb

In Secret Number 1, we looked at the extraordinary power of the telephone as an apartment leasing tool. Our telephones enable us to convey information and goodwill to a huge spectrum of apartment renters in the marketplace. They allow us to communicate genuine concern for helping people find apartments that best match their needs and desires. And they help us begin building a level of commitment that hopefully will result in both another leased apartment and another satisfied resident.

Now we move to the next step in the leasing process. For years, we have heard that "first impressions are lasting impressions," and that "you never get a second chance to make a good first impression." From a customer relations standpoint, it's tough to argue with the wisdom in those words. The importance of making a positive first impression when we first greet our prospects still holds true as one of the most significant moments in the relationship building process.

Each of us has had situations in life where we've experienced the power of first impressions. Yours may have been at a wedding reception, a dinner party, a special company meeting, or a class reunion. Put yourself back at the scene. You'd been anticipating the event for weeks. Dozens—perhaps even hundreds—of people were scheduled to attend, many of whom you knew.

Now get the picture clear in your mind. After carefully selecting your wardrobe and polishing your appearance in every detail, you arrive at the big event. As you walk up to the door, you feel the uneasy sensation of butterflies in your stomach, but you take a deep breath and make your entrance.

Unfortunately, there's just one small problem: *You are invisible.*

The room is crowded with people, but you feel completely alone. People look at you, and then look away, as if you do not warrant their attention. You fight back a wave of anxiety, wondering if there's a glaring flaw in your appearance that you somehow overlooked. Swallowing your pride, you attempt to strike up a conversation, and then another, but for some unknown reason the conversations just shrivel up and die. In short, you're being ignored. And it's enough to make you want to turn around and leave.

Being ignored in social situations is a bitter pill to swallow. But think about this for a moment: How many apartment shoppers walk into leasing offices and experience the very same thing? How many of them encounter those same butterflies, or that same sting of self-consciousness? How many of them are made to feel like an interruption, or an unwelcome intrusion? How many of them, upon walking through our doors, feel ignored—and would rather leave than stay?

BUILDING AN ATMOSPHERE OF ACCEPTANCE AND TRUST

One of the most fascinating aspects of apartment leasing is the endless parade of different people that walk through your doors. Some appear to be pictures of success and self-confidence. Others look and sound as if their world is falling apart. Regardless of how a person may appear to be

dealing with life on the outside, there are almost always heavier issues being dealt with on the inside.

That is why it's important to make the leasing office a place where people can receive attention, acceptance, and trust. Moving is stressful enough by itself, but in many cases it can be even more difficult than usual. While in the midst of a move, some people struggle through the emotional devastation of divorce. Others battle with fear brought on by illness or financial hardship. Still others feel lonely and homesick, as they move away from family or friends. People renting apartments today face the same tough challenges that the rest of us do. And when they come to you, many are hoping to meet a friendly and compassionate person—someone to greet them warmly and to help them lift their spirits.

However, winning the trust of apartment shoppers can be difficult. Over the years, the apartment industry has given people plenty of reasons to withhold their trust. For instance, as an industry, there is a tendency to lie. Much apartment advertising on the market today makes claims and creates illusions that are either terribly misleading or simply not true. Another example is the reputation this industry has for pressuring people with manipulative sales tactics, the worst offender of which is known as the "urgency close."

As a result, it is no surprise that people are reluctant to trust us. Many have learned from previous experiences to be wary. They've been ignored, misinformed, and pressured by us in the past. Therefore, we must all work together toward reversing this trend. We must be on the lookout for wary people, and put forth our best efforts to earn their acceptance and trust.

Winning the trust of cautious apartment shoppers can be achieved in large part by greeting those you meet with warmth, interest, and genuine concern. However, in order to succeed, you need to develop a greater awareness of what we'll encounter in the process. As you prepare to greet and welcome prospects into your leasing office, keep the following principles in mind.

Look for distrust. Many times you can spot distrust right away. Distrustful people have a cautiousness about them. They keep their distance. Their tone of voice may be abrupt or impatient. They can be hesitant to answer questions honestly or in detail, because they're instinctively

on guard. For all they know, you may be just another fast-talking, high-pressure "closer" that will disappear when the deal is done. You can't blame them. If you were in their shoes, chances are you'd feel the same way.

People develop distrustful attitudes over time, usually as a result of repeated attempts by others to take advantage of them. If too much mistreatment occurs, the walls of distrust can grow tall. As salespeople, there will be times when we must exercise a great deal of patience to lower those walls of defense. From now on, watch for signs of distrust in your prospects. Remember that if you're honest, and outwardly concerned about helping people get what they want, you'll stand a much better chance of breaking down the walls between you.

Acknowledge the fragile nature of trust. The level of trust between two people can be compared to a delicate crystal vase. Besides being beautifully and carefully made, fine crystal is also very fragile and costly to replace. Let's say the vase represents trust between you and a prospect. As long as that trust is treated with consideration and respect, its value is enjoyed and appreciated by all. But if it is handled carelessly and dropped, it will shatter into hundreds of pieces. No matter how hard you may try to repair it, it will never be restored to its original unbroken condition.

Trust is arguably the most important element in a relationship, whether personal or professional. It is built upon foundations of honesty, integrity, loyalty, and commitment. If those are the qualities prospects see in you when they meet you face to face, then you can be sure of this: In your lifetime you will acquire many friends, and you will enjoy years of success.

Remember that YOU are the company. When someone walks into your leasing office, who do they see? The owners of the property? The management company executives? The corporate office staff? Occasionally, but not very often. In most cases, they see *you*. You alone are the company to the person off the street.

What this means is that prospects entering your offices are going to draw impressions about the *entire company* based on their encounters with you. If the encounter is favorable, they are likely to rate the company the same way. If it is unfavorable, there's a strong chance that neither they nor anyone else they know will do business with you or your company in the future.

When you first greet a prospect face to face, there's much more at stake than just the occupancy of your community. The fate of other properties in your company may also hang in the balance. Therefore, you must personally assume the responsibility for projecting a professional and trustworthy image of your company. Its reputation in the marketplace depends on how you present yourself to the public.

In summary, the degree of trust people feel when you first greet them has a tremendous bearing on whether or not they lease from you. You must do everything in your power to be seen as trustworthy and reliable representatives of a trustworthy and reliable industry. Making the leasing office a place where people can experience acceptance and trust is the very first place to start.

RELAXING AND BEING YOURSELF

When it comes to serving the public like you do, it's important that you relax and be yourself. If you try to impress people with sophisticated airs, you run the risk of driving them away. This is not to minimize the importance of looking and behaving professionally. It's just that there is a difference between *acting* professional and *being* professional.

Acting professional is superficial. Movies and television continually bombard us with stereotypes of how "sophisticated" businesspeople supposedly act. Unfortunately, good role models are pretty scarce on the screen. Arrogance and self-involvement (the opposite of what we want to project in the leasing office) seem to prevail as character traits in Hollywood's mostly imaginary world.

Being professional, on the other hand, is much more natural. It's also much easier. It springs forth from a warmer and friendlier attitude, regardless of our appearance, income level, or business environment. Being professional—treating customers in precisely the same way we like to be treated ourselves—is a refreshing difference that people immediately notice and appreciate.

Taking a personal interest in our prospects and allowing them to see that we're human does more to strengthen our leasing effectiveness than a sophisticated attitude ever could. Real people like to do business with

other real people. That's the bottom line. What's more, prospects are more likely to lease an *average* apartment from someone they *like* before they'll lease an *exceptional* apartment from someone they *don't*.

In short, it is pointless trying to be anyone or anything but yourself. Most of us eventually discover that we're happier when we stop trying to be people we're not. So, when you greet your prospects, relax and let them see the real you. Until people see the real you, you're not likely to see the real them.

MOMENTS OF TRUTH

In case you are wondering, you read it right—*moments* of truth. A common misconception about the on-site greeting process is that it begins the moment we first look our prospect in the eye, shake their hand, and welcome them into our office. One of the most important facts about the initial greeting is that a prospect's "first impression" when they meet us face to face is usually *not* the first impression they've drawn.

In his book *The Only Thing That Matters*, Dr. Karl Albrecht discusses a concept first introduced by Swedish management consultant Richard Normann. Normann observed that people don't go around thinking about our businesses all day like we do. They only think about us when they have some sort of contact with us, either directly or indirectly. These points of contact are what Normann described as *moments of truth*.

Moments of truth are the various points in time where prospects draw impressions and form opinions about a business—in our case, apartment communities and the professionals representing them. However, many of these impressions are formed before prospects ever meet us face to face. Albrecht thus broadened Normann's definition of moments of truth to describe *any episodes in which the customer comes into contact with an organization and gets an impression of its service*.

Here's how the process typically unfolds: A prospect's journey to your door begins when they see an ad in the marketplace, or receive a recommendation from someone they know. Next, they pick up the phone and give you a call to find out if you deserve a closer look. Provided your telephone presentation keeps you in the game, they get in their car and drive out to see you. As they draw closer to the entrance, they begin to see your signs, flags, banners, decks, patios, lawns, flowers, A-boards, balloons, and so forth. All of these make up the *initial* set of "first impressions" your prospect will experience.

Then the prospect actually drives onto the property. Now they see the parking lot—cars, dumpster enclosures, curbs, oilspots, striping, the works. Then they notice the lawns and landscaping, the condition of the buildings, the entrance to the leasing office, the mailbox kiosk, and in many cases the pool area. Next, they get out of their car, walk up the sidewalk, open the office door, step inside, and immediately experience a whole new set of impressions and sensations. Finally their eyes meet yours, as you walk up to do what: Make a *first impression*? Hardly.

At every step of the way, between the first time they hear about you until the time they meet you in person, prospects draw impressions and conclusions about the quality of your apartments and your service. For example, if a prospect notices a glob of deflated helium balloons draped over your A-board and trash throughout your parking lot, what are they most likely to assume? One conclusion they might draw is that when things need to get done—whether it's picking up trash or completing maintenance requests in their apartment—the staff is slow to act. On the other hand, if they see carefully groomed landscaping and an immaculate leasing office entrance, they will be more inclined to believe that yours is a community worth doing business with.

MOMENTS OF TRUTH IN APARTMENT LEASING

People form their initial opinions about apartment communities based on a wide range of variables that make up a community's overall image in the marketplace:

- Reputation
- Advertising
- Landscaping
- Parking and common areas
- Telephone presentation

- Office exterior
- Signage
- Office interior
- And last, but certainly not least, the leasing office staff.

In sales, customer perceptions are often larger than reality. If your prospects encounter unfavorable moments of truth, like garbage in the parking lot or shoddy landscaping, it won't matter if you have the most wonderful residents in the world. It won't matter if you offer the best customer service in town. Nor will it matter if your floorplan designs are second to none. If the impressions your prospect draws before meeting you are unfavorable, then their perception of your entire community, at least in the beginning, is likely to be unfavorable as well.

The lesson to be learned is clear: There is far more to making good first impressions than immediately meets the eye. Prospects coming through your door experience multiple "moments of truth," in many cases long before they ever reach out to shake your hand.

PREPARING TO GREET YOUR PROSPECTS

Much has been written about how to greet the customer in the apartment leasing business. Here's a classic:

- Stand to greet
- Be friendly
- Shake hands
- Introduce self
- Ask customer's name
- Fill out guest card.

Sounds just about perfect—if you're a robot.

Okay, so it covers the basic mechanics. But a gracious, customer-oriented greeting goes far beyond the scope of a simplistic recipe like this. Customers don't act like robots. Why should you?

Before we discuss the finer points of extending a warm and friendly greeting, let's first discuss how and what we should prepare in advance of that all-important first encounter:

- First inspect all street frontage areas of your property. Be absolutely certain that they are clean, green, and well maintained in every detail.
- Next, check the condition of all other paved and landscaped areas. Concentrate on the areas adjacent to your main entrance, in front of the leasing office, and along the routes to model and/or vacant apartments you intend to show. Beware of relying solely on maintenance or groundskeeping personnel to assume this responsibility. While their involvement is unquestionably important, they may not yet have acquired your same degree of marketing perspective.
- If cluttered decks or patios are plainly visible, contact the residents in those apartments immediately and insist that these areas be cleared (it is critically important to consistently enforce regulations related to storing items on decks or patios).
- Inspect "target locations" (furnished models and market-ready vacant apartments) well in advance of the time when your office opens for business. If at all possible, you want to minimize the chances of running into nasty surprises like hot or cold apartments, live or dead bugs, smelly garbage on a doorstep, and so forth.
- Once these areas have passed inspection, turn your attention to the leasing office itself. Be sure to have refreshments on hand. Fresh seasonal beverages (coffee/tea, cocoa, or spiced cider in cooler months, and lemonade or iced tea during warmer months) are most always well-received. Snacks such as cookies and hard-wrapped candies can be good choices, though in our increasingly health conscious culture you might be better off choosing low-fat snacks (like pretzels) or sugar-free candy instead. Even if refreshments eventually seem dull and routine, remember that they are almost always a welcome treat for people visiting your community for the first time. Also, pleasant aromas (like almond or vanilla) and soft instrumental music in your leasing office do wonders to create atmosphere and enhance the tone of your greetings.
- Have brochures and business cards readily available, as well as community newsletters (if you publish them) and other items of

interest like renter's insurance brochures and furniture rental information. Guard against displaying apartment rental publications in your leasing office. Prospects waiting to see apartments at your community may pick up rental magazines, browse through them, find an ad they like better, and leave without so much as saying a word.

- If expecting the arrival of prospects with whom you've already spoken on the phone, take a moment to review the notes written on their guest card before they arrive. Refresh their names, priorities, and preferences in your mind so that you can greet them with enthusiasm and familiarity.

YOUR APPEARANCE MAKES AN IMPACT

It has been said that when you see a poorly dressed person, you notice their clothes. But when you see a well-dressed person, you notice the person. Though no one ever said it was fair, prospects almost always judge us first by our outward appearance.

Dress codes in the apartment industry are extremely diverse. They often depend on a person's position, range of responsibilities, the time of year, and so on. If you're responsible for painting and cleaning apartments in addition to leasing, then wearing a business suit clearly would not be practical. On the other hand, if your role is exclusively leasing and customer relations, then wearing casual attire is likely to put your community at a distinct competitive disadvantage.

While there are exceptions to every rule, it is almost impossible to overdress in the leasing office. Many apartment shoppers planning to commit $3,000 or more to a lease agreement are looking for (and probably even *hoping* for) a professional-looking person with whom to do business. Unfortunately, prospects often encounter people in leasing offices whose appearance does little to inspire their confidence. T shirts, visible tattoos, revealing blouses or miniskirts, worn-out shoes, knit ties, flashy jewelry, piercing (other than ears), heavy makeup, and powerful aftershaves or perfumes are viewed by many as unprofessional. When our appearance runs contrary to established professional standards, we risk jeopardizing our credibility in the marketplace. If that happens, it can become more difficult to earn the trust and acceptance we need.

What you wear and how you look speaks volumes about who you are and the company you represent. Furthermore, your appearance is the mirror-image of your credibility in the leasing office. When you look your best, chances are that you feel more confident. And when you feel more confident, you project more positive attitudes when greeting prospects at the door. Make every effort you possibly can to polish your appearance. Doing so may literally mean the difference between winning business—and losing it.

SECRETS TO WARM AND FRIENDLY GREETINGS

At this point, let's assume that everything is perfectly in place: The exterior areas of your property are immaculate, the models and vacant apartments are spotless, your office is warm and inviting, and you look terrific. Before your next prospect walks through the door, spend some time reviewing the following secrets to warm and friendly greetings.

Let your enthusiasm shine. There's something extraordinary and unforgettable about genuinely enthusiastic people. They transmit a magnetic, captivating energy that is almost impossible to resist. When you greet your prospects with enthusiasm, you send a message that you like who you are, like what you do, and enjoy helping others get what they want. If you need more enthusiasm in your approach to leasing, commit *right now* to becoming a more enthusiastic person. Letting your enthusiasm shine can be the edge that permanently places you among the ranks of the industry's superstars.

Stand up and move out from behind desks or tables. When we enter a place of business, nothing says. "You're an interruption" faster than a salesperson who remains seated and does nothing to acknowledge our presence. Amazingly, some people in our industry would rather sit and shuffle paperwork than get up and greet someone walking through the door.

Remaining behind a desk also sends a subtle message of power and authority. It's almost as if you're saying, "I'm in charge here, and you're on my turf." You want to avoid creating an atmosphere where you are viewed as superior. Nor do you want your prospects to feel subordinate. Rather you want to offer an environment where everyone feels comfortable and equal.

When a prospect walks into your office, **STAND UP!** Even if you're on the phone, stand immediately and acknowledge the presence of your guest. Then, step out from behind your desk, or wherever else you may be seated, and move forward to meet your prospect. Focus on eliminating all barriers, physical and otherwise, that may exist between you and them.

Introduce yourself by name. Generally speaking, we tend to regard people who introduce themselves to us as friendlier and more professional. Prospects see things from much the same perspective. People who confidently introduce themselves usually get noticed more quickly. In addition, people who confidently introduce themselves invariably make more friends.

When you introduce yourself to newcomers by name, it establishes you as a friendly and outgoing individual. It also creates an opportunity for the other person to introduce themselves in reply. Even more, it immediately establishes a spirit of goodwill between you that did not exist before. If building quick and friendly rapport with others is your goal, introduce yourself by name.

Obtain your prospect's name. In his book *How To Win Friends and Influence People*, Dale Carnegie observed that ". . . a person's name is to that person the sweetest and most important sound in any language." The sound to which we respond most quickly is none other than the sound of our own names.

To illustrate how powerfully we're affected by our names, let's suppose for a moment that you're attending your company's Christmas party. You're engaged in an interesting conversation with a co-worker when all of a sudden you overhear someone at the next table say your name. What happens? In an instant, you stop concentrating on *your* conversation, and start trying to eavesdrop on *their* conversation, because you know that someone else is talking about you. Your entire focus changes on the dime, just with the mention of your name.

Perhaps even more significant is the power we attribute to people who can remember and refer to us by name. Most of us gravitate toward people who know and call us by our names, because they make us feel noticed and important. The ability to associate names with faces is among the most valuable leasing skills you can ever acquire, and the best way to acquire it is through reinforcing your prospect's name in your mind.

Sometimes, though, people don't automatically respond with their name when we introduce ourselves. If your prospect is someone with whom you've never spoken before, here's an effective greeting technique for increasing the odds of getting their name: Introduce yourself by saying, "Welcome to Orchard Terrace! My name is __________, and you are . . . ?" When your question trails off at the end, people will most often fill in the rest of the sentence with their own name. And then you'll have it, to use throughout the rest of your conversation.

REMEMBERING PEOPLE'S NAMES

You can improve your ability to remember names by using two time-tested methods for strengthening your memory and recalling names more consistently. The first is to silently repeat your prospect's name *three times* immediately after hearing it (repetition is one of the best ways to drive a person's name deep into your memory). The second method is to say that person's name in conversation as soon as the opportunity presents itself. When you speak people's names out loud, your chances of remembering them become much better. Also, if you had spoken to this prospect on the phone before they arrived, then you should also have their name on a guest card or an activity log. The point is this: The more you repeat and review a person's name, the more likely you are to remember it.

While we're on the subject of people's names, it is also very important that you say them with respect. For example, you want to be sure that you pronounce them correctly in the form that people prefer (not all "Susans" like being addressed as "Sue"). Moreover, you don't want to abuse people's names, as some telemarketers do when they insert the names of their

prospects into canned scripts. Addressing a person by name has a special way of strengthening their loyalty toward you. So whenever appropriate, use a person's name correctly, conversationally, and with respect. Without a doubt, the sound of a person's name truly is the sweetest sound they know.

Be aware of what you say with your eyes. What goes through your mind when you meet a salesperson who is reluctant to look you in the eye? When you ask them a question, they look away. When they reply, they look away again. Pretty soon, you start to wonder: "Why won't this person look at me? What exactly is he telling me? Or more important, what exactly *isn't* he telling me?"

We communicate powerful messages about ourselves with our eyes. They can tell others we are confident and self-assured. They can also tell others that we are afraid, or that we have something up our sleeves. Sometimes, the messages we send with our eyes are so powerful that they override the messages we send with our words.

In a typical conversation, people exhibit two different types of eye contact behavior. One occurs when we speak, and the other occurs when we listen. When we speak, it is normal for us to occasionally look away from our partners, breaking eye contact while we think up the words we want to say next. Put another way, the speaker's eye contact is naturally somewhat erratic. When listening, however, it is better to maintain steady eye contact with whoever is speaking to you. If you don't, the speaker is apt to assume that you are bored, or that you don't care about what is being said. A very important part of being a good listener, therefore, is maintaining eye contact with people when *they* speak to *you*.

American business culture places a high premium on steady eye contact. We associate it with character traits like honesty, credibility, and self-confidence. All of these qualities are what future residents look for in a leasing professional—qualities that are more often than not reflected in our eyes.

Smile. What a difference a smile can make. In our modern media culture, we're continually bombarded with bad or aggravating news. Sad though it is, watching the nightly anchors or reading the daily headlines can be enough to wipe the smile off anyone's face.

But then, on the one day that you think you just can't handle any more of the world's heavy baggage, a total stranger passes you on the street and smiles. At *you!* All of a sudden things look wonderfully different. Your faith in humanity rebounds. And you realize that it doesn't seem like such a bad day after all.

A genuine smile isn't just something we do with our mouths. Smiling, like enthusiasm, is a special expression of goodwill that comes from within. A genuine smile radiates first from our hearts, and then from our eyes, and eventually illuminates our entire presence. It lights up our words and warms the hearts of others in a way that few other things can.

Nobody needs a smile so much as the person who has none left to give. Remember, a heartfelt smile is one of the most encouraging and inspiring gifts that there is. Difficult though it may be, strive always to meet each day with positive energy and good cheer. Welcome every prospect that comes through your doors with the brightest smile you've got, and see if you aren't amazed at the ways in which people respond.

Think about your handshake. A firm handshake as part of the initial greeting can be one of the more effective moments in the entire encounter. A lot of important characteristics are communicated about a person through their handshake—confidence, goodwill, and integrity, among others. However, a number of other traits can be communicated as well, like aggression, nervousness, or a lack of genuine interest.

In most cases, shaking hands as part of a professional greeting is a natural and expected thing to do. However, for some people shaking hands may be uncomfortable. Many senior citizens suffer from the painful effects of arthritis, which can make handshaking an unpleasant experience. Then there are people who wear large or numerous rings, which may cause pain when pressured by a strong grip. Still other people are so shy and introverted that a firm, assertive handshake may intimidate them more than anything else.

The point is that there are times when you should stop and think before shaking someone's hand. In the majority of cases, a firm handshake gets things off to a flying start. But there are exceptions. Be watchful, and if you feel that a handshake may cause your prospect either physical or emotional discomfort, leave it out of the greeting equation.

Acknowledge those who must wait. Many times, especially on days when you are the only person in your office, prospects and residents alike are forced to wait for service. Even when people have appointments, you can't always guarantee that you won't be occupied with something or someone else when they arrive. But remember—people walking into your office don't really care about your circumstances. They care about *theirs*, and few things in life are more frustrating than having to wait.

If you are serving another person when a prospect walks in, *make sure* that you acknowledge the presence of your new arrival. Make them feel noticed, and reassure them that you'll assist them as soon as you are able. If you are on the phone when someone walks in, once again *stand up* and make eye contact with whoever has come through the door. Motion them in, direct them to an available seat, and periodically assure them of your intention to serve them as quickly as possible.

This brings up an innovative solution to greeting prospects when you are occupied on the phone. Rather than offering the usual flurry of hand signals or silently mouthing a bunch of incomprehensible words, you can do something far more creative—and far more effective:

Prepare a printed message that you can show people who must wait until you're off the phone. Copy it onto colored paper, then laminate it for durability. When people come into your office and see that you're busy with a call, motion them over and show them the message. Here's an example of what it might say:

> *"Welcome to Highland Ridge! I'll finish this call as soon as possible, so that I can give you my undivided attention. In the meantime, please make yourself comfortable, and thank you for your patience!"*

What you want people entering your leasing office to know is that their presence is important to you. Using a sign like the one just described is yet another extra-mile approach you can use to better tell your customers "You matter." So whatever you do, be it verbally or some other way, promptly and cheerfully acknowledge anyone entering your office who may have to wait.

Use a "message board". The whole idea behind a warm and friendly greeting is to shower your prospects with attention and make them feel like honored guests. Message boards are a distinctive manner in which you can add even more impact to the impressions you create when prospects walk through your door.

One popular style of message board is the pedestal-mounted type often seen in hotel lobbies and at entrances to restaurant dining rooms. These boards are used to display messages, which are created by affixing white plastic letters to a black felt background.

You can use a message board of this type to create remarkable first impressions. First, if you're expecting a prospect who has scheduled an appointment by phone, you can spell out a personalized greeting that makes them feel like a star from the moment they walk in. Fifteen minutes before they arrive, prepare a message on the message board that says something like this:

> ***"Washington Hills Is Proud to Welcome***
> ***Chris Wilson.***
> ***Our #1 Goal Is to Serve You!"***

In addition, you can use your message board to acknowledge new residents on their move-in day:

> **The Staff at Washington Hills**
> **Is Pleased to Welcome**
> ***Chris Wilson***
> **As Our Newest Resident.**
> **Welcome Home, Chris!**

When people walking through your door see their names front and center, they're going to feel wanted and important. And that, of course, is precisely how you want them to feel. So try using a message board. They are an inexpensive and attractive addition to your leasing office; some sell for under $50, complete with the letters you need. When you see the delight on people's faces, you'll know that your investment is paying off.

LAYING THE FOUNDATION FOR FUTURE SUCCESS

The initial greeting is an extremely important step toward gaining a prospect's trust and establishing a positive rapport. And while your ultimate objective is to have that person lease an apartment, there's a great deal of getting acquainted that needs to take place first. Look at the greeting process as a way to set the stage for future success. Don't be too quick to shove a guest card into people's hands, or to immediately launch your presentation. Whenever possible, take your time. Try to relax, and help your prospect relax as well. Let a friendly conversation develop and take its course. Make people feel so warm, so welcome, and so important with your greeting that it becomes virtually impossible for them to resist your offer of help.

REVIEW

Before greeting a prospect for the first time, remember to:

- Build an atmosphere of acceptance and trust. Do this by working to put distrustful people at ease, and by recognizing the fragile nature of trust.
- Relax and be yourself. People want to see the real *you* before they show you the real *them*.
- Recognize that your prospect has already formed a perception of your community before ever meeting you face to face, as a result of experiencing *moments of truth*.
- Before your prospect arrives, thoroughly inspect and prepare all exterior and interior areas yourself. Don't rely solely on maintenance or groundskeeping staff; you probably know what your prospects will notice better than anyone else.
- Consider the impact your appearance has on people's attitudes toward you and your community. What you wear and how you look speaks volumes not only about who you are, but also about the company you represent.
- Keep in mind the secrets to warm and friendly greetings:

Let your enthusiasm shine
Stand and move from behind desks or tables
Introduce yourself by name
Obtain your prospect's name
Be aware of what you say with your eyes
Smile
Think about your handshake
Acknowledge those who must wait
Use a "Message Board"

- Lay the foundation for future success. Make people feel so warm, so welcome, and so important when they enter your office that their decision to lease is virtually assured.

Secret Number 3

Stop "Qualifying" Your Prospects and Start Interviewing Them

Relationship selling is the state-of-the-art today. It means custom-tailoring information to individual people.

Brian Tracy, motivational speaker

Most people working in apartment leasing offices today were taught from the beginning to "qualify their prospects," almost as if the process of interacting with prospects were a one-way street. It's surprising that this antiquated approach has gone unchallenged for as long as it has. Who do we think we've been kidding? In this era of increased competition and consumer sophistication, prospects qualify *us* every bit as much as we qualify *them*.

The time has finally come for the apartment industry to move away from using the term "qualifying." It just doesn't fit the nature of what we do. Frankly, traditional qualifying is a customer-*un*friendly process. It is interrogatory, and it is cold. Besides, it tends to focus more on financial considerations than it does on the equally important lifestyle and emotional factors that figure into a person's decision to move. While yes, we must carefully assess an applicant's income, credit, and rental history before handing them a key, the last thing we want is for legitimate prospects to feel like they are required to pass some sort of "suitability test" before we'll lease them an apartment. As leasing professionals, we must continually remind ourselves that it is *our* job to earn the *prospect's* business—not the other way around.

That is why I refer to the initial meeting between leasing staff and prospective residents as the *leasing interview*. The process should not be an interrogation, where the leasing consultant assails the prospect with an avalanche of questions. Rather, it should be a conversational sharing of information with one goal in mind: Helping the prospect find an apartment that uniquely meets his or her needs. *That* is what we are paid to do.

Let's pick up where the greeting left off, and assume that a genuinely interested person is now standing in your office feeling welcome and at ease. The leasing interview—where first you gather, then share relevant information with your prospect—can now begin.

IN THE BEGINNING . . .

The secret to successful leasing interviews is to begin them in a conversational and friendly way. Too many leasing professionals make the common mistake of shifting into a business-like selling mode immediately after greeting their prospects, which is an issue we'll discuss further in a moment. Before beginning the interview process, it helps to raise our awareness of certain things we'll encounter along the way.

Expect indifference from your prospects. A common tendency among leasing professionals is what I refer to as "approval addiction." As salespeople, we tend to like it best when prospects are as nice to us as we are toward them. But sometimes they aren't. Sometimes we encounter prospects who treat us with cool indifference. When we do, we have a tendency to conclude that they don't like us, which can cause us to act cold or indifferent in response. And if we aren't careful, walls of defense can quickly rise up on both sides.

No matter how charming a person you may be, not everyone who enters your leasing office is going to show you their approval. Some

people are just indifferent. Not only that, they've probably got things on their minds other than being nice to you. But don't be discouraged. Remember, this person is in the process of committing thousands of dollars to a lease, which is enough to preoccupy even the friendliest of personalities. So give people the benefit of the doubt. Expect indifference. That way, when you experience it, you'll know that it isn't necessarily because of you.

Keep your personal agenda out of sight. It's no secret that you get paid to lease vacant apartments. Everybody knows it, including your prospects. They are fully aware that if they lease an apartment from you, it is likely that you will be compensated for it.

However, that doesn't mean you should make it obvious. In fact, what you stand to gain if you lease the apartment is completely unimportant to the prospect. They don't care about what you get. In fact, they probably don't even want to *know* what you get. All they care about is what *they* get.

That is why you must keep your agenda out of sight. No matter how desperate your vacancy situation may be, always keep your motives for leasing apartments to yourself. Prospective residents honestly do not care what you will get if they lease. As long as you help them get what they want (which is an apartment that meets their needs) they will help you get what you want. And that, of course, is a lower vacancy rate.

Take the lead. Whether you realize it or not, your prospects view you as a leader—an expert in the apartment industry. Before they even step foot through your door, most of them have made an assumption: They are about to interact with a person who can help them make a good decision.

Think about it—we start out as capable leaders in the eyes of our prospects before we've even said a word. That's quite an advantage. However, one of two things can happen at that point. We can either destroy their initial regard for us as leaders, or we can promote and build upon it.

Let's examine the worst-case scenario first. The fastest way to destroy a prospect's regard for you as a leader is to ignore the need for preparation. People not only expect you to possess the knowledge and information they need, but they also expect that you'll be able to explain it in a way that makes sense. What's more, many of the people who walk through your door aren't sure what they want. These people need you to *lead* them in

the direction of a good decision. If you're not prepared to discuss specifics about your apartments and translate them into how well they match our prospect's preferences, we will have failed in our leadership role. Worse, the prospect's problem of finding the right apartment will remain unsolved.

On the other hand, building credibility as a qualified leader requires a solid foundation of product knowledge and preparation. Genuine leaders in apartment leasing study the details about their apartments and their communities until they know them backward and forward. They regularly practice their sales presentations with friends and co-workers. They observe prospects closely, watching for leasing signals and listening for feedback from which they can learn. They research their competitors carefully, and religiously monitor responses from their advertising and marketing campaigns. All this advance preparation enables them to increase their skill at matching specific prospects with specific apartments at precisely the right moment—much like fitting a hand in a glove.

It's been said that the best way to know whether or not you're a leader is to count the number of people following you. If people lease apartments from you, then you clearly possess the ability to lead others in making good decisions. If no one is leasing from you, do not despair. Hope is not lost. The issue probably lies less in your natural ability than it does in the degree to which you have prepared. If your desire is to become a person who can confidently lead others, commit yourself to preparation. Make up your mind to become a person others can rely on for capable direction. When you do, you'll be amazed at the number of people who enthusiastically act on your advice.

Be seated and establish a cordial atmosphere. When you watch leasing experts in action, you'll notice that they rarely begin a leasing interview by talking about apartments. They understand that prospects often feel anxious when they walk into a leasing office, and anxious people are known for being resistant. Therefore, instead of rushing headlong into their presentation, experts first go out of their way to make their prospects feel comfortable.

In the leasing interview, a gradual and more relaxed beginning is much better. While this is not to say that you should hesitate in getting

things underway, you need to give both yourself and your prospects a chance to adjust. Upon greeting your prospect, graciously invite them in. Offer them refreshments. Treat them like you would a special guest in your own home.

Then, lead them to an area where everyone (including yourself) can be comfortably seated. If you don't have a designated customer seating area, do everything within your power to create one. Circular arrangements seem to work best for leasing interviews, because in a circle there is no seat of authority. Seated around in a circle, everyone is on equal ground. However, if the chairs in front of your desk are the only seats available, do this: When prospects come in, pull your chair out from behind the desk and seat yourself out front, on *their* side. A well-balanced seating arrangement does wonders for putting people at ease.

Now relax. Start things off with a bit of friendly conversation about your prospect's day, their kids, the new car they pulled up in . . . anything that places them at the center of attention. Create a cordial and comfortable atmosphere. Before anything else, make sure people know that you are interested in *them*—and not just their signature on the dotted line. The opportunity to talk about the business of leasing them an apartment will come soon enough.

GATHERING INFORMATION FROM YOUR PROSPECTS

You objective in the leasing interview is to gather information about your prospects that will help you understand:

- What they want most in an apartment home.
- How the apartments you offer match what they want.

The information and insights you gather in the interview are extremely valuable. However, there is a problem. Most of us are better at *gathering* information than we are at *using* it. The real-life story you're about to read will illustrate.

Karin (not her real name), like many in our business, was trained to obtain completed guest cards from every prospect she could. When a prospect walked into her office, Karin's response was automatic. After greeting them warmly, her standard operating procedure was to hand them a guest card and ask them to fill it out.

One day, a nicely dressed gentleman walked in. Karin greeted him and, following her usual routine, handed him a guest card. She excused herself to retrieve a set of keys, switched her phones over to the answering service, and returned. By this time, her prospect had completed his guest card.

Taking it from him, she led him out the door and began walking toward a model of the apartment type he wanted to see. About halfway across the parking lot, the man stopped Karin and asked her a question that nearly killed her on the spot.

Here's what he said:

"Why did you make me fill out that card? You haven't even looked at it."

Karin was absolutely mortified, but the guy was right. She had reached a point in her leasing experience where she viewed the guest card as just another piece of paperwork instead of as a way for people to share important details about themselves. She was doing a terrific job of gathering the information. She just wasn't using it.

It is interesting to note that Karin is a veteran in our business. Make no mistake: She is an outstanding salesperson. In fact, she's so good that she was able to recover from her embarrassment and lease the apartment after all. She learned a hard but valuable lesson that day, and to her credit was honest enough to share the experience for my benefit and yours. We must remind ourselves daily that if the information we gather is important to our prospects, it ought to be just as important to us. If people take the time to share it, we must take the time to use it.

USING GUEST CARDS

Karin's experience aside, the value of using guest cards in the leasing interview cannot be overemphasized. They are the best tool we have for capturing information gathered during the leasing interview. In addition, guest cards are invaluable when we need to refresh our memories or make more notes as we're demonstrating an apartment. They provide us with

one of the most reliable means of documenting the effectiveness of our advertising investments. And, they are essential to maintaining a consistent follow-up program.

Guest cards can be obtained through a number of sources, most notably from companies that publish apartment advertising publications. In many cases, these companies provide guest cards to their advertisers free of charge. If you've never used guest cards and would like to start, contact a rental advertising magazine publisher or apartment association in your area. If they can't provide you with guest cards, they should have a good idea who can.

Guest cards can be used *whenever* there's an opportunity to gather information from an interested prospect. That opportunity may come to you in person. Or, it may come to you over the phone. Don't make the mistake of using guest cards only for in-person visits. They are equally effective for recording prospect information during telephone presentations. As we saw in Secret Number 2, the notes you record on guest cards while on the phone will enable you to greet your prospects with familiarity once they arrive. In addition, those same notes will help save time on both sides by eliminating the need to repeat your initial phone conversation.

Sample Guest Card: Front

Welcome to Our Apartment Community!

Name ______________ **Today's Date** ______________

Address ______________

City ______________ **State** ______________ **Zip** ______________

Phone Numbers: Daytime ( ) ______________ **Evening ( )** ______________

E-Mail Address ______________ **Best Time to Contact** ______________

Employer ______________ **Position Held** ______________

Annual Household Income ______________ **Price Range** ______________

Size of Apt. Desired ☐ Studio ☐ 1 bdrm ☐ 2 bdrm/1 bath ☐ 2 bdrm/2 bath ☐ 3 bdrm

Date Needed ______________ **Number of Occupants** ______________

How did you find out about us?

☐ Driving by ☐ Rental magazine ☐ Newspaper ☐ Friend ☐ Locator ☐ Other ______

Sample Guest Card: Back

For Use By Office Staff		
Type of contact ☐ Telephone Inquiry ☐ In-person visit **Leasing Rep. initials** ____		
Size/type of apt. shown ________________ **Apartment #'s**______________		
Specific needs & preferences ________________________________		
Questions or concerns ________________________________		
	Follow-Up Record	
Date	**Comments**	**Initials**
________	____________________________	________
________	____________________________	________
________	____________________________	________

Feel free to use this format, if you like.

There has long been a debate over who should fill out the guest card: the prospect or the leasing consultant. Though again there are always exceptions, the most customer-friendly policy is to complete the information for the prospect. There are three reasons for this approach: One, it's something you can do to serve the prospect right up front. Two, it better ensures that you'll get all the information you need about them. And three, it gives you an opportunity to work in concert with one another.

Here's how the process works: Start by taking the lead. Tell your prospect that you want to find out more about them and what they're looking for. Then ask their permission to take down a bit of information. When they agree, pull out a guest card, record their name, ask them the Magic Questions, and simply fill in the guest card as they respond. As secret 1 pointed out, there may be a few details that the Magic Questions do not bring to light. If that is the case, ask whatever additional questions might be necessary (yes/no or Six W's) to balance out the information.

Keep in mind that we may not always have time to complete guest cards in this fashion. In fact, sometimes we may have to ask prospects to complete the guest card themselves. If this becomes the case, just remem-

ber that apartment shoppers can find guest cards irritating, especially when they've shopped numerous communities and have grown tired of filling them out. If *you* were shopping for an apartment and nine leasing consultants in a row shoved guest cards under your nose to fill out, by the time number ten rolled around you'd probably feel a little irritated yourself. So do your prospects a courteous favor. Complete the guest card for them. The vast majority will appreciate the gesture as thoughtful and service-minded.

WHAT INFORMATION DO YOU NEED FROM YOUR PROSPECTS?

Following is a list of the key information you need to learn about your prospects, including but not limited to:

Their name and address
Phone numbers for home and/or work
The type of apartment they want
Their price range
The expected number of occupants
Their desired move-in date
Whether or not they're employed, and with whom
How they found out about you
Whether or not they have pets

Guest cards provide space for gathering most of this information. However, many of the more important details you need—like what things are most important to the prospect, where they are living now, and the reason they are moving—may not be addressed within the guest card format. That's why it is so important to ask the Magic Questions and make additional notes as the interview unfolds.

Once again, your objective in the leasing interview is to gather as much information from a prospect as you can, in order to better understand and serve their needs. But the leasing interview serves another purpose as well. It is what enables you to talk in their terms. Remember—if I'm your prospect, I'll get bored if the things you say don't include or relate to me. The only way you're going to lease me an apartment is to make me feel important and unique. The way you'll do that will be to describe an apartment in terms of what matters to me most. And the only way you can possibly find out what's most important to me is to *ask*.

Information-gathering skills, along with a willingness to listen, are vital components of a successful leasing interview. You can strengthen your abilities in both areas by consistently using guest cards and asking good questions. Combined, they will produce a wealth of information you can use later when demonstrating the apartment.

DOMINO QUESTIONING

There is another questioning technique you can use to gain more information once the interview process is underway. It is known as *domino questioning*, named after the chain reaction created when a line of dominoes is stood on end and the first one is tipped over.

Just like the first falling domino acts upon the next in line, one question influences the next in domino questioning. One question raises an issue, which raises another more specific question, and before you know it an interesting conversation begins to develop. The process begins with *primary questions*, moves next to *secondary questions*, and then continues with *exploratory questions*.

Primary questions. Primary questions are what we use to get the leasing interview rolling. They give you a "big picture" of what your prospect wants. The best primary questions are, of course, the Magic Questions. People respond to them with remarkable ease and they almost always produce a wide range of the important details you need.

Secondary questions. Secondary questions help clarify statements generated by your primary questions. A good way to phrase secondary questions is to begin them with *why*. If a person answers a primary question by saying they want a third-floor apartment, but doesn't say why, there will almost always be a reason behind it. Secondary questioning will help you uncover what that reason is; for all we know, it may be a major issue in their mind. Here's an example of a secondary question you might ask: "*Why do you prefer a third floor?*" Now you stand a better chance of reaching the heart of the matter. Other examples might include, "*Why is covered parking important to you? Why do you want beige carpet?*" Or,

"Why do you prefer a southern exposure?" As you can see, the secondary line of questioning encourages your prospect to reveal more of what's on their mind, and the more information you can get, the easier your job will be.

Exploratory questions. Sometimes we have to dig a little deeper for the things we need to know. That is where exploratory questions come in. The reasons people give in response to secondary questions can oftentimes be vague. Let's say that when you ask a primary question, your prospect tells you they want an energy efficient apartment. Okay, great. Now for the secondary question—*why* is that important? Let's say they respond this time by telling you they're on a tight budget. Better, but not a whole lot more enlightening. What could be happening is that they're paying a fortune to heat the apartment they're living in now.

Asking an exploratory question can help you find out for sure. An effective way to phrase exploratory questions is to begin them with *what*. Here's how you might use the exploratory question in this scenario: *"What experiences have you had with heating bills in the past?"* Now the prospect has an opportunity to tell you what's really going on. Now you have a better chance of getting somewhere.

As you'll see in the next chapter, information like this can do wonders for helping you match apartment benefits to your prospect's individual needs.

To summarize, all you have to remember about domino questioning is this: Primary questions are simply the Magic Questions: *Describe for me*, and *tell me about*. (See Secret Number 1.) Secondary questions begin with *why*. And exploratory questions begin with *what*.

Let's have Lisa come back and demonstrate how domino questioning works as she sits with Bill in her office and proceeds with the leasing interview.

Lisa: I've reviewed the information we discussed over the phone last week (which is when she asked the Primary/Magic Questions), and I think I've got a pretty clear picture of what it is you're looking for. But just in case, is there anything else that you'd like to have in your new apartment?

Bill: Well yes, now that you mention it, *I'd really like to be on the top floor*.

Lisa: Okay, let me add that to the list. If you don't mind me asking, **why is a top floor important to you?** (secondary question).

Bill: Well, I guess I'd just be happier. I lived in a middle floor apartment one time and it was a nightmare.

Lisa: ***What happened?*** (exploratory question)

Bill: Well, there were these two yahoos that lived upstairs from me . . . (proceeds to tell Lisa the story).

Lisa: Wow. I'm sorry to hear that. I can really appreciate what you're saying. In fact, some of our most satisfied residents—people who incidentally live in middle floor apartments—told me almost identical stories when they first came here to look. (She then proceeds to share a glowing testimonial from a middle floor resident, which she obtained especially for use with prospects resistant to middle floor locations. Bill remains neutral, but at least seems open to further discussion.)

Lisa: Tell you what—why don't we take a look at the apartment I described to you over the phone? I know you're a little concerned about middle floor locations, and if I had been through an experience like yours I'd probably feel the same way. The apartment I want to show you *is* on a middle floor, but it's got a couple of design features that really help reduce the kinds of problems you've dealt with before. What do you say—shall we go have a look?

Bill: Okay. I guess we could do that.

Lisa: Terrific. This is one of our best apartments. I really think you're going to like it.

Notice that Lisa went straight to the heart of an issue that initially didn't seem like a big deal—until she began asking domino questions to obtain more information. If instead of asking the secondary question she had said, "I'm sorry—all I have available is a middle floor," Bill probably would have made up his mind on the spot: *"I told myself I'd never rent another middle floor again. I hate middle floors. I'm getting out of here."* Then he would have started searching for an excuse to leave.

FINDING YOUR PROSPECT'S EMOTION

Picture this scene:

Two hitchhikers are standing side by side on a desolate, snow-blown stretch of highway. One holds a sign that says, "To Seattle." The other one holds a sign that says, "To Mom's for Christmas."

Who do you think will catch the first ride?

Emotions powerfully influence people's decisions, particularly when it comes to deciding where to live. When most of us think of *home*, we tend to associate it with one or a combination of the following key emotions:

Happiness	Sadness
Kindness	Anger
Security	Fear/Vulnerability
Peace	Conflict
Love	Hate

In most cases, people's decisions to move are driven at some level or another by emotion. However, people rarely select apartment homes based on emotion alone. In an attempt to demonstrate the importance of emotions in the decision-making process, it has been suggested that fully *90 percent* of people's decisions to buy are based on emotion, and that only 10 percent of their decisions are based on facts or logic. But when it comes to leasing an apartment, this simply can't be true. In reality, the ratio is much more balanced, averaging about 65 percent emotion and 35 percent logic.

Here's why. When decisions are based entirely on emotion, they tend to be made in haste. As many of us know from personal experience, hasty decisions often result in *buyer's remorse*, which is something few people enjoy. Additional proof is the fact that buyer's remorse translates into one of the biggest problems we face: *cancellations*. On the other hand, when people base decisions entirely on logic (i.e., numbers and features alone), their decisions tend to be apathetic. They may wind up being the best-educated prospects in town, but they probably won't feel terribly motivated to lease one apartment over another.

In the end, most decisions to lease apartments follow the 65/35 rule. Emotion and logic both play important parts, but when it comes down to

the nitty gritty, a person's emotions are usually what tips the scales. Since emotions are often the most important decision-making variable, you should start your interviews by addressing the factual side of the equation first—what types of apartments you have available, what interior features you offer, whether they have pets, and so forth. Then, as the level of familiarity and comfort increases, you can gradually build toward a more emotional and meaningful approach. As you're about to see, finding a person's emotional "hot buttons" can make a huge difference in whether or not a person ultimately decides to lease.

But here's the tricky part: How do you uncover people's emotions in the leasing interview without being intrusive and arousing resentment? Again, the secret lies in tactful questioning. One technique you can use to reach beyond the surface to a person's deeper emotions is an approach developed by Jim Eeckhoudt known as "why times three."

Why times three. Let's say that you're interviewing a single mother, who has not yet informed you that her ex-husband has been harassing her and her children. As the conversation develops, she says she wants a third-floor apartment. This is where you can use *why times three*. It can help you get to the real issues.

So using the *why times three* technique, the first question you would ask is, ***Why?*** Let's say, not surprisingly, that she gives you a vague response along the lines that she is concerned for the safety of herself and her children. Now it's time for your second question: ***Why?*** At this point, she might say that she's been having some problems with her "ex," again not giving you much detail. But details are what you need if you're going to reach her real emotions. Therefore, you need to ask the third ***why*** question, which might be phrased something like this: "I'm sensing that you feel a little bit threatened. Would you mind telling me ***why?***"

Please don't misunderstand; the intent of this approach is not to pry or intrude. By way of comparison, think for a moment about what doctors do. When you go to them with a problem, they do not hesitate. They immediately start asking questions, which we all know can be blunt and even embarrassing. They can't afford to beat around the bush. There's no reason to. They need to know the details, so they can help us get better as quickly as possible.

As apartment leasing professionals, why times three enables us to take a similar approach. The only difference is that we are helping people with their housing, not with their health. As long as we're polite, sincere, and genuinely concerned when we ask our prospects potentially sensitive questions, the likelihood of offending them is remote. However, if someone does take offense, it's not the end of the world. Just smile, apologize, and change the subject.

Now let's go back to the single mother. For the sake of discussion, let's assume that your approach has been so sincere and gentle that she hasn't taken offense to your questions. She finally tells you the real reason she wants a third-floor location: Her "ex" broke into the first-floor apartment where she's living now and physically abused her. *Now* you know that the primary emotion driving her decision to move is *fear*. Knowing this, you can pour even more of your energies into reassuring her and earning her trust. You can also more effectively tailor your upcoming demonstration to emphasize the features and benefits of a third-floor location that specifically address her need for safety.

Feature	***Benefit***
Double-locking, solid core door	Adds strength
Intercom system	Deters unwanted visitors
Well-lit common areas	Discourages prowling
Neighborhood watch program	Heightens awareness
Nightly "courtesy patrols"	Provides visible deterrent

Without using the why times three approach, you might never have understood which apartment benefits would be *directly relevant* to her. If you had not gained insight into her most pressing emotions, you might have made the mistake of emphasizing benefits unrelated to protection, which was clearly the most important issue on her mind.

In the leasing interview, concentrate first on the factual information that has to be addressed. Next, focus on gently bringing your prospect's emotional motives to light. Finally, present apartment features and corresponding benefits in terms that are relevant to the emotional priorities you uncover. Once again, when you reach people's *emotions*, you reach the *real person*.

PRESENTING INFORMATION TO YOUR PROSPECTS

The leasing interview is a two-way street. While yes, you want to obtain information about your prospects, they want information from you too. As the quote at the beginning of this Secret Number 3, indicates, you want to tailor the information you present so that it's relevant to the prospect you're working with. The secret to presenting information effectively lies in the following key principles.

Talk in terms of your prospect—not yourself. When you begin the leasing interview by talking about yourself or your communities, here's what typically happens: On the outside, your prospects appear interested. They nod, smile, and look as if they're captivated by what you're saying. Don't be fooled; they are not. They're just being polite. On the outside they appear to be saying, "Wow! What you are talking about is really neat!" But on the inside, they're rolling their eyes and saying to themselves "Who cares? This is boring."

When the time comes for you to talk, begin by emphasizing only the apartment and community benefits you know are relevant to your prospect. They may have no interest whatsoever in the horseshoe pit or the nearby bus stop, even though you have those advantages to offer. At some point there may be reason to mention your monthly horseshoe tournaments, but if three bedrooms and a garage are the most important items on your prospect's agenda, address those items first.

However, there is another challenge we often encounter. What should you do if your prospect is the "silent type" who doesn't express an interest in anything? Your only choice in these cases is to do the best you can to *create* some. Take a step of faith, and present the best qualities your community has to offer with passion and conviction. Periodically ask open-ended questions in an attempt to gauge their interest. "How do you feel about activities like the ones we offer?" Or "Why is a downtown location important to you?"

Make an effort to refrain from using phrases like, "We have ***this***," or "Our community has ***that***." It is important that you hold off on telling your story until it can be told in your prospect's terms. If your prospect

should try to initiate the leasing interview by saying "So, tell me about your apartments," be careful. You don't yet know enough about them to present information in their terms. Instead, turn things around with a question that puts them back in the center of the conversation: "Well, there's a lot to tell. Before we go into all of that, though, let's start by talking about *what's most important to you*. Could you take a few minutes and **describe for me** (Magic Question) the things you want most in your new apartment?" Once you have that information, knowing which apartment features and benefits to present—and how to present them—becomes much more clear.

One final note: In the leasing interview, you'll have plenty of opportunities to bite your tongue. Take advantage of them all.

Respect your prospect's time as if it were your own. Have you ever dealt with a rambling, overly talkative salesperson who wasted what little time you had to begin with? It's unbearably frustrating when salespeople ignore our subtle cues of impatience, like checking our watch, scooting forward in our chair, or getting out our keys. Eventually, our frustration can turn to anger, which is most unfortunate for the salesperson. Angry prospects aren't generally in the mood to buy.

Most people are protective when it comes to their time. It is not uncommon for people to decide against purchases because of thoughtless salespeople who ignore the warning signs. When presenting information in the leasing interview, watch closely for indications of restlessness or impatience in your prospect. If those signs should appear, do something immediately to involve your prospect and return them to the center of attention. If you gather the impression that they are determined to leave, don't cause them further delay. Graciously afford them the opportunity to depart.

Hold the brochure. What you are about to read may fly in the face of everything you've ever learned: It is *not* necessary to review a brochure in the leasing interview. In fact, referring to a brochure in your interview may do you more harm than good.

If you're having a conversation with someone, and they suddenly hand you something to read, what do you do? If you're like most people, you look at it and start reading. That's why teachers and professional speakers

carefully time how they distribute printed information to their listeners. They know people won't pay nearly as much attention to what is being said if there is something in front of them to read.

A similar thing can happen in the leasing interview. The conversation moves along at a brisk and engaging pace until the brochure is brought out. At that moment, a flurry of questions flood your prospect's mind. They're not sure which they should do—listen to you, or read the brochure. Even if you point out the things you want them to focus on, it's almost impossible for them to resist reading and thinking about things you haven't yet discussed.

Pretty soon, that flurry of questions begins to come out, and all of a sudden you find that you're not asking the questions anymore; your *prospect* is. Instead of leading, you're now following. Instead of talking about them, you're now talking about *you*, and you know what happens when you wind up talking about yourself. It's just a matter of time before the prospect begins to think, "Who cares? This is boring."

By all means, if your prospect picks up a brochure and starts looking at it, don't yank it back out of their hands. Just subtly draw their attention away from it. Ask questions. Keep them talking. You want them connected to you—not to your brochure. There will be plenty of time to review brochures later. For now, keep the conversation on track. Leave your brochure out of the interview, and concentrate instead on building the conversation.

Begin dramatizing your ideas. The more entertaining and interesting you are when presenting information to your prospects, the more excited they will become in what you have to offer. When describing key information about your apartment benefits, do *everything you can* to present that information with drama and flair. A single dramatic statement about what your prospect will gain is worth 50 mundane facts about the apartments themselves. Use gestures. Be creative. Expand your vocabulary. Be *different*.

Make it your daily challenge to describe apartment or community details in the most colorful and intriguing terms you can. Paint vivid verbal pictures for your prospect. Let them see themselves victoriously achieving their fitness goals on the stairclimber, or pulling their car into

a dry, well lighted garage. Help them visualize *all* of their clothes hanging together in your humongous walk-in closets. Create a descriptive snapshot of them lounging on the pool deck, iced tea in hand, on a bright and balmy summer day. Get them into the interview. Produce a "mental motion picture" that places them in the starring role.

BECOMING A PERSONALITY TO REMEMBER

Which types of people excite and motivate you the most? People who look and talk like wooden statues? Or people who radiate energy and creative ideas? All it takes to develop a more dramatic interview style is a moment of self-evaluation. Close your eyes and imagine yourself in a prospect's shoes. Ask yourself, "If I were a prospect, would I be interested in listening to me?" If the answer is no, then you must concentrate on increasing your energy and using more of your imagination. If the answer is yes, congratulations—but don't get complacent. You must always keep looking for fresh and innovative ways to present your ideas. The more dramatic you can be, the more memorable you and your leasing interviews will become.

REVIEW

The leasing interview should be a comfortable, two-way process that allows both you and your prospect to determine how well your apartments fit what they're looking for. In the beginning stages of the leasing interview

- Expect indifference from your prospects.
- Keep your personal agenda out of sight.
- Take the lead.
- Be seated and establish a cordial atmosphere.

When gathering information from your prospects

- Use guest cards. While there may be exceptions, it's generally best to complete guest cards for your prospects. Recognize that the guest card is an extremely important component of the leasing interview process.

- Use *domino questioning*—primary, secondary, and exploratory questions—to obtain additional information in the leasing interview. Good primary questions are the *Magic Questions*. Secondary questions typically begin with *why*. Exploratory questions most often begin with *what*.
- Achieve a better understanding of the emotions driving your prospect's decision by using Jim Eeckhoudt's "why times three" technique. Remember that when you reach people's emotions, you reach the real person.

When presenting information to your prospects

- Talk in terms of your prospect—not yourself.
- Respect your prospect's time as if it were your own.
- Hold off on reviewing brochures in the leasing interview. Keep your prospect focused on you.
- Finally, begin dramatizing your ideas. Present everything you say with as much flair and creativity as you can. Ask yourself, "If I were my prospect, would I be interested in listening to me?"

Secret Number 4

Involvement Is the Key to Dynamic Demonstrations

*Tell me, and I may forget. Show me, and I might remember. But **involve** me, and I'll understand.*

Chinese proverb

Leasing consultant to prospect, as they enter a vacant apartment:

"This is our two bedroom, one bath. It's about 850 square feet (long pause, while prospect glances around). *It's got beige carpeting, separate living and dining areas, baseboard heaters, brick fireplace. Do you like to build fires?"*

Prospect says, "Sometimes."

Our leasing consultant continues. *"It's got a sliding glass door out onto the patio, where there's an adjoining closet for extra storage."* (Points to closet through the glass.)

Prospect nods, affirming that she does in fact see the storage closet.

"Over here (consultant moving along) *is the master bedroom. It's real good size, about 12′ × 12′ square . . . big closets, too."* (Prospect nods.) *"And back this way is the bathroom."* (Consultant switches on

the light and expertly flicks a dead fly off the countertop, hoping it will go undetected.)

Faintly smiling with amusement, our prospect glances at the bathroom—and the fly.

"Down this way is the second bedroom. It is smaller than the master, but you'd be amazed at the stuff people manage to squeeze in."

Prospect looks it over for all of about five seconds.

"Last, but not least (directing the prospect back toward the front door) *is the kitchen. Dishwasher, self-cleaning oven, lots of cupboard space. . . ."*

Prospect nods again.

Then our leasing consultant "goes for the close." *"This apartment rents for $525. We take first, last, and a $300 security deposit, $100 of which is nonrefundable. What do you think?"*

If you were evaluating this leasing consultant's performance, what would *you* think? As distressing as it is to say, the preceding demonstration can be summed up in one word: *Typical.*

PREPARING TO MAKE A DYNAMIC DEMONSTRATION

The previous scenario is not just a figment of the imagination. It is the way that hundreds, and probably thousands, of apartments are "demonstrated" every day. No drama. No imagination. No opportunities for prospect participation or involvement. Just a room-by-room tour, where the obvious is boringly and mechanically pointed out.

Secret Number 4 is devoted entirely to elevating apartment demonstrations from the ho-hum to the dynamic. But before we can ascend to new heights of demonstration skill, we must again return to the sharpening stone of preparation. Just as it pays to prepare for telephone presentations, greetings, and leasing interviews, it also pays to prepare in advance of demonstrating an apartment. Before you set foot in a vacant apartment with a prospective resident, make sure you cover the following bases:

Assemble a "community information notebook." Just as experts in construction or medicine use tools in their trades, we must use tools in

ours. The leasing consultant who carries a notebook filled with detailed information about their apartments, their competitors, and their most desirable neighborhood conveniences enjoys a tremendous advantage in the marketplace. The reason is simple: Prospects tend to regard salespeople who are visibly equipped for the job as better qualified to render the service they want. When you carry a community information notebook, you inspire confidence in the hearts of apartment shoppers. It shows that you're qualified to lead them in making a good decision.

So what's the secret to preparing a community information notebook? Begin with a three-ring binder, equipped with at least five tabbed divider pages. Here's practical, easy to follow notebook format, along with a variety of ideas for items you'll want to include

Tab One–*Community Maps*

Site maps are a valuable reference resource to include in the notebook. They should be color-coded to show the location of your leasing office, various floorplan types on the property, carpet colors, furnished model(s), laundry centers, recreational areas (pools, playgrounds, ball courts, etc.), water and gas shutoffs, fire hydrants, guest parking areas, and the like. If you decide to assemble this much information, you may be better off making several copies of the site map. Designate one to show your different floorplan types, another to show carpet colors at those locations, another to show the location of laundry centers and recreational areas, and so on.

Tab Two–*Apartment Specifications*

In this section, include *enlarged* floorplans (not the miniaturized ones that appear in most brochures) illustrated with square footage and important room dimensions; construction data (date built, width of exterior walls, floor construction, type of windows, etc.); insulation ratings (or *R values*) of floors, ceilings, exterior walls, and windows; instructions for operating heat controls, fireplaces, and/or air conditioning systems; explanation of circuit breaker diagrams; and so forth.

Tab Three—*Neighborhood Information*

Here you'll want to create a comprehensive summary of as many neighborhood advantages as possible. This list should include addresses, phone numbers, and any other relevant information for the following area conveniences: child care centers; elementary, middle, and high schools; area colleges and universities; mini-storage centers; grocery, home improvement, and department store shopping; freeway access ramps; churches; parks; movie theaters; car washes; gas stations; video stores; popular restaurants; banks; health care facilities; libraries; post offices; bus stops; and so on.

Tab Four—*For New Residents . . .*

In this section, compile information that new residents may need: telephone numbers for police, fire, and medical services in addition to 911; numbers (and perhaps even contact names) for local telephone service providers and cable television companies; the number for your local power or gas company in the event you don't set up utilities service for new residents; and so forth. You may want to visit your local post office for free copies of their *Moving Guide*, which contains change of address forms and other helpful moving tips. You might also create a "moving checklist" customized to your specific community. This checklist could remind your new residents of their need to notify friends and relatives, credit card issuers, insurance agents, banks, the post office, etc., of their move.

Tab Five—*Comparables*

The last section of your notebook is where you'll want to keep updated information about your primary competitors. The information in this section should be organized on what is commonly known as a "comparable market survey" form. Many, if not most, property management companies have their own version of this. Usually in the form of a spreadsheet, it designates areas for listing key characteristics of your property and other properties comparable to it (sample shown on page 73).

Many times prospects will indicate that they've been looking at other apartments in your area. They may mention certain things they like or dislike about your competitors. Regardless of what a prospect may say,

Date: _/_/_	Our Community			Comparable Property			Comparable Property			Comparable Property		
Name												
Address												
Telephone												
Management Company												
Age/Number of units												
Occupancy												
Market Rents	Avg. Rent	Sq. Ft.	$/Sq. Ft.	Avg. Rent	Sq. Ft.	$Sq. Ft.	Avg. Rent	Sq. Ft.	$/Sq. Ft.	Avg. Rent	Sq. Ft.	$/Sq. Ft.
Studio												
1 + 1 Efficiency												
1 + 1 Standard												
2 + 1												
2 + 2												
3 + 2												
Current Concessions												
Required Deposits												
AMENITIES												
Pool/Spa												
Fitness Center												
Tennis/Racquetball												
Clubhouse												
Washer & Dryer												
W & D Hook-ups												
Laundry Facilities												
Cable												
Controlled Access												
Courtesy Patrol												
Pet Rents/Deposits												
Other												

Comparable Market Survey

NEVER sling mud at the competition. Instead, let the facts in the Comparables section of your notebook speak for you. Don't attack your competitors' weaknesses. Just focus on selling your strongest benefits. If other apartments your prospect is considering really are comparable, then their final decision will probably boil down to which leasing person does the best job of earning their trust and respect.

Let's wrap up our discussion on community information notebooks with a few more important points. You may want to include information other than what is listed here, and that is great. The more, the better. But whatever you do, strive to create a notebook of distinctly professional quality. Use a computer to format as much of the information as you can. Remember—some people will request copies of it, and any materials you give to people directly reflect how you define quality. In addition, current residents may benefit from the information you gather as well.

So be generous. Make copies available to anyone you think would find the information helpful.

The highest reward you'll gain from using a community information notebook is a greater degree of self-confidence; you'll be able to satisfy your prospect's information needs faster and more accurately than ever before. Once you create it, don't be caught on a demonstration without it. Use it to strengthen your professional image, and to better inform the prospects you serve.

Study your competitors. If there's any hope of making the cut with prospects who have done their homework, you'll have to know your competition inside and out. As you're demonstrating the apartment, your prospect will likely be comparing everything they see—including you and your style of demonstrating—with your trusty competitors down the street. If those competitors are assertive and customer-oriented, as some of them undoubtedly are, then you can rest assured that they'll do everything in their power to see that your prospect leases from *them*, and not from you.

The very first prerequisite of preparing to make effective apartment demonstrations is to understand your competition. Even if you pull off an Academy Award–winning demonstration, it could be blown sky-high if the

prospect is more sold on a competitor than they are on you. The only way you can prevent that from happening is to be well-enough prepared to "sell around" your competitor's strengths. If you can't, chances are very good in the end that your prospect will conduct a demonstration of their own—a demonstration of loyalty—to the competition.

If you're not devoting at least two hours per week to visiting and evaluating your competitors, you cannot sufficiently prepare yourself to compete in tough market conditions. **No matter what it takes, schedule time every week to study your competitors.** And don't waste your time looking for what they're doing wrong. It's okay if they're doing the wrong stuff; that's what you want them to do. You need to concern yourself with what the competition is doing *right*. The better you understand the strengths of your competitors, the stronger and more competitive you will become.

Inspect approach routes to furnished model and target vacant apartments. After preparing the information you'll need on the demonstration, it is vitally important that you inspect the routes you'll be walking throughout the day *before* your first prospect arrives. It's amazing what mysteriously appears on sidewalks, lawns, and stairways in the middle of the night.

Your goal should be to minimize, if not completely remove, things that might turn people off on the way to see an apartment. Smelly garbage, bikes and toys, "carpet scrap" doormats, mangled landscaping, and pet waste are prime examples. If necessary, request authorization to have front doors painted, stairwells pressure-washed, and hallways swept or vacuumed. Make sure that exterior and common area lighting fixtures are clean and operable. If you must pass by unpleasantries like sloppy or disorderly residents or barking dogs, create a top-priority action plan for addressing, documenting, and resolving those issues at once. As best you can, make sure the approaches to every apartment you plan to show are clean, green, and free of nasty surprises.

You should allow at least a half hour to inspect your routes before opening the leasing office. If your office hours begin at 9 a.m., don't begin inspecting at 9:00. If your office hours begin at 9:00 a.m., you should begin your daily inspection procedures *no later than* 8:30, so that you're completely ready for business by 9:00. Leasing professionals who travel this extra mile almost always enjoy the highest occupancy levels in the mar-

ketplace. Doing anything less is inviting the unexpected—and asking for trouble.

Inspect furnished model and market-ready apartment interiors. Apartments that are on the market and available for occupancy should be inspected every day. Though this may seem excessive, it's the only way we can keep from growing complacent, and in apartment leasing, complacency is the kiss of death. Therefore, the standard for apartment quality that we must all strive to meet is this: Every apartment into which we take our prospects must be *market-ready*. The following definition is extremely important:

Market-ready apartments are *completely ready* for occupancy.

Market-ready apartments do not need to be painted. They do not have draperies that are waiting to be hung. Nor do they have carpets that still need to be cleaned. A market-ready apartment, if not new, has been restored to as near-new a condition as humanly possible. Besides completing the paperwork and conducting a move-in inspection, there should only be two things left for you to do before the prospect moves in. One is taking their money. The other is handing them their keys and welcoming them home.

At this point, you may be saying to yourself, "Now wait a minute. If I only have one vacant apartment and someone insists on seeing it, I'm going to let them see it—even if it isn't market-ready. They'll just have to use their imagination." Not so fast. You're playing with fire. In fact, consider this not entirely improbable scenario:

You're on a vacation that took you months to save for and plan. One evening while on the road, you locate what appears to be a nice hotel and check in. You're in a hurry to unpack and relax; however, room service is still in the process of preparing your room. Even though the room is not "market-ready," you insist on getting the key. The front desk clerk reluctantly agrees.

Bags in hand, you arrive at the door and walk in. The first thing you notice is the bare mattress, or rather the stains that are on it. Empty beer cans litter the floor. There's a musty, half-eaten apple in the garbage can. Then you step into the bathroom. You see a toilet that has not been

flushed. You see the bathtub, its drain clogged with hair. Everywhere you look, you see someone else's dirt.

Bet you can't wait to settle in.

The details in this example, however disgusting you may find them, are included to illustrate a critically important point: No matter how good a job the housekeepers may do, it will be virtually impossible for you to get the dirt you first saw out of your mind. Similarly, unless an apartment is absolutely ready for a prospect to view or occupy, they are more likely to remember what *isn't* ready than what *is*. Please, please, please: *Do not show dirty apartments, under any circumstances!*

Every day, before inspecting apartment interiors, examine the appearance of all exterior areas. Think of what your prospects will see; how they feel about the apartment interiors will be influenced by how they feel about the property exteriors. Start by making sure that trash and pet waste are picked up, parking lots and walkways are swept or blown, and so forth.

Next, move to your furnished models, if you have them. See that lights are turned on, climates are comfortable, and that "atmosphere" has been created with music and aromas. Finally, market-ready vacant apartments should be carefully inspected and spot-cleaned, if necessary. Carpets should regularly be vacuumed or raked. Footprints left from previous demonstrations can suggest to incoming prospects that there has been a lot of traffic through the apartment—but for some reason, nobody has wanted it. And, as we're about to see in the next section, vacant apartments should be creatively accessorized for maximum marketing appeal.

Every apartment you present to the marketplace must be in as close to brand-new condition and as appealing to the five senses as you can possibly make it. If they aren't, you run the serious risk of getting beat out by competitors who hold to higher standards and put forth more effort.

A final point about apartment preparation is that fancy models and clever accessories aren't what lease apartments.

Leasing professionals lease apartments. All the gimmicks in the world won't matter at all unless we first establish positive relationships and heighten people's interest in what you have to offer. The ability to effectively relate with people comes before *anything else* in the overall formula for leasing success.

Accessorize market-ready apartments. You might think of the vacant apartment you have to show as a blank canvas. Would a person shopping for a painting buy a blank canvas? Of course not—they'd buy a finished work of art. They'd buy it because of the way it made them feel, and the way it appealed to their senses. In the same way, market-ready vacant apartments should be creatively accessorized for maximum sensory appeal. An accessorized vacant apartment, or what is referred to as a *target vacant*, is much more likely to increase a prospect's interest than if it were left "blank."

Setting up "targets" is one of the most creative and entertaining ways to dramatically increase your closing ratios. Look for the liveliest, most inexpensive things you can find to give vacant apartments color, energy, and five-sense appeal. Use plug-in wall fresheners or scented sprays to create pleasing fragrances (studies have suggested that vanilla and almond are among the most appealing aromas). Hide small radios and tune them to instrumental or soft rock stations. This helps to both create atmosphere and mask noise from adjoining apartments or the outside. Put balloons, package-wrapped boxes, colored or scented hangers, and laundry products in closets. Splash festive confetti and streamers on countertops.

Use multi-colored balloons throughout. Buy small houseplants, with imaginative cards to go alongside that say something like, "Put Down Your Roots with Us!" Hang stockings over the fireplace at Christmas time. Put food in the freezer, beverages in the refrigerator, and notes on the door that say, "Look inside!" Find humorous doorhangers for bedrooms and bathrooms. Place a dish of specialty soaps in the bathroom; accessorize it further with a brightly colored shower curtain, new hand towels, a toilet lid cover, and so forth. (One other tip on bathrooms: To prevent prospects from asking to use the restroom in your model apartments, remove the bathroom doors. Once a person sees that the bathroom has no door, they'll instantly realize that they'll have to wait.)

Another high-impact idea is to produce "Apartment Inspected By" tent cards for placement on counters or breakfast bars. Any printed displays in a vacant apartment are guaranteed to get read. Take advantage of this phenomenon by creating tent cards that convey both your standards for quality and the readiness of the apartment itself. Here's an example:

ASSURANCE OF QUALITY

This apartment has been carefully serviced and has been found to meet the standards for quality and cleanliness set by

[*property or management company name]*

Your complete satisfaction is guaranteed by

____

(signature of leasing, maintenance, and/or housekeeping personnel)

The ideas listed here barely even scratch the surface of the things you can do. There is *absolutely no limit* to the ways in which you can accessorize a vacant apartment. Let your imagination run wild. For less than $100 you can take a bleak, silent apartment and transform it into a high-energy environment that people will remember. One secret to dynamic demonstrations is to make them FUN—for both your prospects and yourself. Setting up target vacants is a wonderful way to do exactly that.

Make sure your keys work. There are few things so embarrassing as stepping up to a doorway, prospect in tow, and discovering that your keys won't work in the lock. You might as well turn and shout to the world, "I AM NOT PREPARED!"

Yes, mistakes happen, but failing to have the right key is perhaps the most preventable mistake there is. Inspecting your models and target vacants beforehand ensures that the keys you're carrying will get you and your prospects where you want to go, when you want to go there. The last thing you want to do is march your prospect all the way *back* to the leasing office for the right key. Aside from it being a frustrating and embarrassing delay, there's no telling what surprises might occur as you backtrack.

While we're on the subject of keys, the use of master keys by leasing and maintenance personnel is rapidly becoming a thing of the past. Many properties have had them lost or stolen, and a master key on the loose is a crisis with absolutely nightmarish implications.

Therefore, if you and your co-workers are currently carrying master keys, it would be wise to stop. Not only is it safer for your residents, it is also safer for you. Set up a separate keybox specifically for keys to your models and vacant apartments. Rotate keys in and out of the main keybox as apartments are vacated or leased. With a minimum of effort and organization, you can set up a system that will help prevent the unthinkable—a master key in the hands of a criminal.

AS YOU LEAVE THE LEASING OFFICE . . .

Let's back up for a moment to the final stages of the leasing interview. When the interview reaches the point where your prospect agrees to see an apartment, you then need to decide which apartment (or apartments) to demonstrate. There's an important point to consider about how you make that decision, and how you present it to the future resident.

Offer your prospect a choice. The apartment industry is closely scrutinized for discrimination against persons belonging to legally protected classes. Directing prospects to certain apartments and not to others based on their race, color, religion, sex, national origin, handicap, or familial status is an illegal practice known as *steering*.

Most apartment leasing professionals would never dream of illegally steering a prospect. Nevertheless, it happens (or is alleged to have happened.) That is why you must take extra precautions not to steer anyone wanting to see an apartment.

One way to avoid steering, or even the appearance thereof, is to offer your prospects a choice of apartments to see. Near the end of the interview, determine which of your available apartments best fit your prospect's preferences, and then describe for them the ones you have in mind. You might say something like this: "Let me tell you about a couple of apartments I have that best seem to fit what you're looking for." After providing brief descriptions, ask which *they'd* like to see first and take them to their first choice. (It is strongly recommended that you document all conversations and activities with prospects, whether they're members of protected classes or not. At this time, the responsibility for protecting yourself and your company from liability due to violations of the Fair Housing Act appears to rest squarely on the shoulders of the leasing office staff.)

Again, if you need more information about the Fair Housing Act and general guidelines for compliance with it, contact the U.S. Department of Housing and Urban Development (HUD) office nearest you.

Make personal safety a priority. Not long ago, a serial rapist stalked leasing offices in the greater Seattle area. He would pose as a prospect, then attack female leasing professionals once he had them inside a vacant apartment.

It is vital that the apartment industry emphasize the issue of personal safety as a top priority for leasing professionals. Following are some safety tips, taken from some of the most experienced leasing professionals in the business, that you can use to better protect yourself on the front lines.

- Request photo identification from *every person* wishing to see an apartment. You might further insist on *government-issued* identification (like a driver's license, passport, or military ID) as the only form accepted. Make sure that you post your ID policy in plain view to minimize questions and reduce your exposure to charges of discrimination. Requiring photo identification before demonstrating apartments can be an effective way of discouraging people with dishonest or criminal intentions.
- If you're not already using them, urge your supervisor to invest in two-way radios (walkie talkies). These are a good way of openly displaying your security priorities to the public, and they can enable you to remain in contact with the leasing office while out demonstrating on the property. If nothing else, should you be assisting a prospect who seems peculiar, be sure your co-workers know exactly where on the property you are going. Better yet, use the "buddy system." Establish subtle codes in the leasing office to signal when you want a co-worker to accompany you with the prospect or meet you at the apartment you'll be showing.
- When demonstrating, continually maintain an escape route in case things take a turn for the worse. **Always allow your prospect to enter the apartment first.** As you follow them inside, if the door has a deadbolt feature, throw the bolt while the door is open so that it cannot swing shut. Another excellent idea is to invest in a supply of rubber doorsteps. Keep one behind the door of each market-ready apartment you show. When entering the apartment, prop open the door with the doorstop. Explain that doorstops are included free

with each apartment to make moving furniture and unloading groceries easier, and don't feel obligated to explain further. Only someone with ulterior motives would seriously object to an open door.

- Once inside the apartment, subtly continue to remain positioned for escape if necessary. Without being obvious, remain between your prospect and the exit door at all times. NEVER place yourself in a position where you could be cornered. For example, walk-in closets are wonderful benefits to demonstrate, but to the criminal mind they're a perfect trap for unsuspecting victims. Never enter closets or tight spaces ahead of prospects. And as a general rule, allow prospects to enter rooms first. Once inside you can still direct the demonstration, but you're in a much better position to run for the door if someone tries to assault you.
- If at all possible, do not demonstrate apartments after dusk.
- Reserve the right to refuse service to people you believe are under the influence of alcohol or drugs. Even if an intoxicated person later chose to file a charge of discrimination, it would be better defending yourself against them in a court of law than it would be trying to defend yourself against them in the isolation of a vacant apartment.
- Bottom line, listen to your instincts. You're under no obligation whatsoever to remain in situations where you feel vulnerable or threatened. If your intuition tells you that you're in danger, and your gut tells you to run, don't stop to think about the financial or legal consequences. **RUN**! If you have to explain, apologize, or testify later, so be it. At least you'll be safe and out of harm's way. *That's what matters most*.

Keep the dialogue moving. Now let's return to your prospect. You've studied your competitors, inspected all approach routes and market-ready apartments, checked your keys, offered your prospect a choice of locations, and developed a "safety first" mindset. Out the door you go.

At this point in the process—when you are walking from the office to the apartment—conversations have a tendency to falter. The last thing we want to do is walk across the property in silence. However, in order to fill lags in the conversation, leasing professionals sometimes make the mistake of falling into the "let's see, what can I tell you about next" routine. If

things stall, try to keep the conversation brisk and customer-focused. Continue asking genuinely open-ended questions, such as:

What kind of work do they do?
What major projects might they be involved with?
Have they traveled recently? If so, where, and why?
What are their favorite hobbies or forms of recreation?

Like we saw in Secret 3, it is *not* necessary to "talk apartments" as you leave the leasing office. (Although I'm not saying you shouldn't. If people start asking questions about the apartments or the community, by all means tell them what they want to know.) However, it's just a matter of time before you encounter "the silent type" who simply will not say anything. When dealing with silent types, volunteer information about your apartments or the community, and then follow with open-ended questions. Initiate conversation about *them*. And relax. If they still won't communicate, at least you'll know you've tried.

Finally, as you talk with prospects on the way, be completely honest. If someone asks about something objectionable, like neighborhood crime rates or noise from the freeway, don't sidestep the issue. Be a professional, and while doing your best to be positive, give them a straight answer. It's better to be up-front, and let people decide what they will, than to be viewed as dishonest or deceptive. Also, if you know there is a key issue that may be a problem—for example, your prospect owns a boat and you don't allow RV parking—it's *your* obligation to bring it up. In the long run, honesty and disclosure (with discretion, of course) are always the best policies.

Stay in step. Sometimes nervous energy causes us to walk faster than we normally do. As a result, we can wind up ahead of our prospects, talking over our shoulders as they follow.

While sometimes sidewalks or pathways are too narrow for people to walk side by side, do your best to walk next to your prospect from the leasing office to the apartment. If that's not possible, walk closely behind and direct them to other person/your destination. Your goal as you walk must be to continue establishing that all-important foundation of trust. If there's a wide physical distance between you, friendly rapport and trust may take longer to develop.

Show vacant apartments before you show furnished models. While there's been much debate on this issue, and again there are exceptions to every rule, prospects should be taken to available vacant apartments *before* they're shown furnished models.

The reason is much like the one illustrated by the dirty hotel room analogy. If I'm your prospect, and you take me into a lavishly furnished model apartment that's never actually been lived in, I'm going to be enchanted by that atmosphere. I'll savor the fragrance of potpourri. I'll hear the soothing sounds of instrumental music. I'll admire the unblemished carpet, the flawless countertops, and the fireplace that's never been used. This is the first impression of your apartments I'll place in my mind. Anything else I see will be consciously or subconsciously compared to it.

After seeing the model, let's assume that you take me into a vacant apartment. Imagine my disappointment when I see that *this* apartment, even though it's been made as market-ready as it can be, has burn marks on the kitchen counter. There's a bleach stain on the carpet near the laundry closet. The inside of the fireplace is blackened with soot, and its glass doors are discolored from the heat. The rooms smell faintly of cigarette smoke. There's no sound! There's no color! There's no fragrance! There's no life!

The picture in this hollow, empty apartment doesn't fit the picture I saw at first. I don't want this one. I want a *nice* apartment, like the model.

If you're fortunate enough to have a furnished model, *demonstrate your* ***vacant*** *apartments first*, so that your prospects won't be dwelling on pristine qualities they cannot have. After demonstrating the vacant apartment, take your prospect to the model for ideas on arranging and accessorizing. Save your best for last. Finish strong. You'll keep your prospect from experiencing "visual letdown" caused by aesthetic differences between your model and vacant apartments.

WHAT'S YOUR OPENING LINE?

Finally—the big day has arrived. From the time you picked up the telephone, days ago, you've been working toward this moment. Picture the scene: You're walking up the stairs, laughing with your prospect about a

funny comment she made. You take out your key, slide it into the lock, and presto—it works. You turn the knob, and the door starts to open. Just as you're about to direct her inside, it hits you:

What do I say now?

If you've ever had this happen, you're not alone. All of us have had experiences where our brains disappeared into thin air. While these things do happen, we want to make sure they don't happen very often. We want to be prepared with opening lines that have meaning and impact, so that our momentum never falters.

"This is our two bedroom, one bath . . ." is *not* an effective opening line. It is nothing more than a statement of the obvious. It presents no imagination. It addresses nothing of particular interest. In short, it's pretty much completely worthless.

Great opening lines are ones that *heighten anticipation* for what your prospect is about to discover. The best way to create a dramatic opening line is to select a detail that your prospect has mentioned about themselves, or an item they have mentioned an interest in, and use that as the foundation for your opening comment. For example, your prospect might have mentioned that they have a lot of plants. One possible opening line based on this particular bit of information could be this: As you open the door, say, "Wait until you see the light in here! Your plants would absolutely grow like wildfire." Or you might say, "The natural lighting in this apartment would be ideal for a person with lots of plants."

As we've seen so far throughout this book, anything you say that doesn't include your prospects will bore them. "This is our two bedroom, one bath . . ." doesn't include anyone. From now on, before you arrive at the apartment, listen closely for preferences and details that you can use to create meaningful opening lines. Also, remember that you want to establish a subtle measure of control before entering the apartment—not over the prospect mind you, but over the *process*. You want your prospects to stay with you during the demonstration. If you're chasing people around an apartment, pointing things out after the fact, you're not in control anymore. You're not leading, like you should be. You're *following*. And if you're following your prospect from room to room, things tend to go from bad to worse.

So be direct. If storage is what a person needs, and you can offer it, enter the apartment by saying, "This apartment has an incredible amount of storage space. Let's start by looking at the outside storage first." Or, if a fireplace is expressed as a preference, say something like this: "You had mentioned an interest in the fireplace. Have you ever been shown how fireplaces like these work?" Then, after allowing your prospect a few moments to take in their new environment, direct their attention to the benefit mentioned in your opening line. While you obviously don't want to boss people around, you do want your prospects to remain focused on the benefits you present. Remember, you're the leader. *Be in charge.*

LET THE DEMONSTRATION BEGIN!

The demonstration is your best opportunity to boost the prospect's interest in what you have to offer. If you build a strong enough foundation of interest and enthusiasm in your demonstration, then people will feel more excited about leasing the apartment they see.

Following are five demonstration techniques that you can use to get people excited about leasing apartments from you. While reading this next section, keep in mind that the secret to expert demonstrations lies in capturing your prospect's interest, and involving them in the process to the greatest extent possible.

Present apartment features in terms of their benefits to your prospect. If you remember nothing else from this book, remember this: Apartment shoppers don't lease apartments. They really don't. They lease what apartments *do for them*. Put another way, they lease the *benefits* that apartment *features* provide. Experts in apartment leasing know that people choose apartment homes based on how well the apartment features will provide benefits to enhance or accommodate their lifestyle.

Sometimes there is confusion over the difference between features and benefits. Why is it important to present apartment features in terms of the benefits they provide? For the answer, let's take a closer look at each.

By definition, a *feature* is a conspicuous or distinctive characteristic. Its appeal is mostly rational. A *benefit*, on the other hand, is something that is helpful or advantageous. Its appeal is more emotional. Notice that

a feature is just a thing; by itself, it doesn't have much meaning. It *becomes* a benefit when it is used or viewed in a way that helps people or gives them an advantage.

Take, for example, a vaulted ceiling. Why would a vaulted ceiling be of value to someone? Certainly not because it increases the square footage of the apartment; vaulted ceilings don't provide functionally usable space. Vaulted ceilings become a benefit when we point out how much roomier they make an apartment *look*, and how much more refined they make the prospect *feel*. Without question, vaulted ceilings create an elegant ambiance in an apartment, which directly reflects on the tastes of the person who lives there. The benefit of a vaulted ceiling, then, becomes a matter of atmosphere and self-image. The ceiling in and of itself has no intrinsic value. Only when presented in terms of its benefits to the prospect does it become an important factor.

There's unbelievable power in selling benefits. Consider McDonald's restaurants. How do they convince us to buy their products? Do they try to sell us on the ingredients, or *features* of their food—fresh bread products, 100 percent American beef, and the finest vegetables money can buy? Of course not. Since most people regard fast food as junk, a features-based sales approach would almost certainly be doomed to failure. Instead, McDonald's emphasizes *benefits*: family fun, speedy service, and affordable prices. They know that most of us will base our buying decisions on benefits before we'll base them on features. As a result, McDonald's strategy of selling benefits over features has enabled them to sell billions of hamburgers around the world.

Another good example can be found in Nike Shoes. There's no doubt that Nike uses the best quality leathers and fabrics available to build their world-famous shoes. The rubber in the soles is second to none. Even the laces are virtually indestructible. But do we ever hear about these features when reading or watching a Nike ad? No, we see *benefits*: healthier bodies, electrifying action, heroic personal achievement, and high-flying performance. Nike knows that its customers aren't just looking for leather, nylon, rubber, and glue. If they can get us to believe that wearing their shoes will bring us the benefits of health, fitness, and excitement, Nike knows we will buy them.

The very same principle holds true when people lease apartments. People don't lease fireplaces, washer/dryers, fitness machines, double-locking doors, or covered parking. They lease romance and energy savings, family convenience, health and improved self-image, relative safety, and peace of mind. If you walk into an apartment and announce that it has brand-new carpeting, a microwave, and walk-in closets, all you're doing is pointing out features. Remember—people don't lease features. They lease *benefits*, which are what features *provide*. The carpet provides comfort and color coordination. The microwave provides time and money-saving convenience. And the walk-in closet provides valuable, needed space. The more you emphasize benefits instead of features in your demonstrations, the more interested and more enthused your prospect will become.

Put your prospect's preferences first. As your demonstration begins, continually remind yourself that your prospect is a completely unique individual, with specific tastes and specific ideas on how things should be done. Frankly, as you demonstrate the apartment, the prospect's way is the only way that matters.

Many leasing professionals—rookies and veterans alike— inadvertently make the mistake of telling their prospects how to arrange a room. While it is good to offer suggestions, try to resist saying things like, "You'll love this apartment! You can put your entertainment center right here, and your dining set right there, and hang a picture like so. . . ." If I'm your prospect, I don't really care what you would do. I might listen, and respond with courtesy, but in the end I'm still going to do things my way.

The best approach is to identify your prospect's preferences and put them first. What kind of furnishings do they have? Or what else might they be planning to buy? Once you find out, begin brainstorming. Have your prospect describe their decor. Ask them, "How do you think you might arrange this room?" By all means, feel free to suggest ideas that have worked well for you or for other residents you know. The key is to *suggest*—you want to avoid creating resentment by imposing your personal preferences on other people. As we've seen, most prospects don't initially care much about you (or what you think, for that matter). They care about *them*, so place them and their stuff at the center of the demonstration.

HOW TO GET YOUR PROSPECTS INVOLVED

The typical features-based demonstration is no more interesting than a mechanical guided tour. Think back to the beginning of this secret: "... *this is the living room, this is the dining room, this is the bedroom, this is the bathroom, and this is the kitchen ... nice, huh?*" Um, no. It is not. As demonstrations go, an approach like this is as boring as they come.

Think of involving your prospects as if you were teaching them to ride a bike. If someone didn't know how to ride a bike, and you wanted to teach them, you could start by giving them all the books you could find on bike riding. Then you could rent videos and together watch dozens of ways to successfully ride bikes. You could even go to seminars where the skills of bike riding were demonstrated. But until that person actually climbed aboard a bike, they'd never learn to ride. Think back to the proverb that begins this chapter. The secret doesn't lie in telling. Nor does it lie in showing. The secret lies in getting people *involved.*

Involving prospects in your demonstrations is not only vital to helping them understand the benefits of an apartment. It is also the critical first step toward asking your prospect to put down a deposit. The easiest way to get your prospect involved is to give them what are known as "minor orders."

Minor orders. Minor orders are not things we ask our prospects to do. They are things we *tell* our prospects to do. Here's how the process works: You describe a benefit, and then tell your prospect to *do something* that will help them understand the value of the benefit. When you give prospects minor orders, you don't have to work as hard; prospects get involved with the process and discover the benefits you want them to see on their own. When their involvement results in discovery of things important to them, they remember. Better yet, they'll *understand.*

Let's say that as you walk into the apartment, your opening line is, "If you've ever wanted an incredible view, wait until you see this!" As you follow your prospect into the apartment, pause for a moment so they can adjust. Then, give them their first minor order: *"Go ahead and pop open the sliding door. We'll step outside for a better look."* What happens? In most cases, your prospect walks over, unlocks the door, opens it up, and out you go. Could you have been polite and opened it for them? Of course you could, but if you show them they *may* remember. That's not good enough. You need to involve them. That's the way you'll get them to visualize. That's the way you'll get them to understand why they should lease.

Once you've stepped out onto the balcony, sell the benefits of the view you now see. Express your enthusiasm for how incredible it really is. Then, let's assume that there's an adjoining storage closet. Invite your prospect to open it up so they can see for themselves how much storage space they'll have. Ask which of their belongings they'd need to store in there. Relax. Listen. Give the prospect time to visualize, and let the conversation happen. Don't concern yourself with talking people into anything. Presented with enthusiasm, benefits convince in ways that artful persuasion never could.

Continue with the demonstration. Suggest that you go back inside. Indicate that next you'll demonstrate some interesting aspects of the kitchen that they're sure to appreciate. *Be in charge*. Make a point beforehand of learning, for example, an interesting technical detail about your icemakers. Ask your prospect to open the door and pull out the tray. Demonstrate the specific feature and corresponding benefit you've learned. Lead them to the point of discovery, and then let them do the "hands on." Interest them. Educate them. *Involve them*, one room at a time.

Incidentally, this is the essence of how an apartment is leased: *One room at a time*. Make sure your prospect is sold on each area of the apartment before you move to the next. As you finish in one room, ask your prospect a form of the following question: *Do you feel like this would work?* Asking this question periodically throughout the demonstration helps you determine at what point your prospect becomes ready to commit. If a certain room won't "work," you may be able to point out ways your prospect could compensate for it. If few or none of the rooms work, you've just saved time and energy for everyone involved. As you demonstrate, monitor your prospect's attitude toward the apartment. Ask questions, listen, and provide benefit-oriented information when the opportunities arise. Watch and measure—one room at a time.

Relate minor orders to benefits. Behind every minor order should be a valid reason. In other words, we shouldn't ask people to do something if

there isn't a benefit in doing it. Asking someone to open a drawer for the sake of opening a drawer is an insult to their intelligence. When you ask people for their involvement, it must be predicated upon an implicit promise that doing so will result in a meaningful discovery.

Imagine that now you've moved from the kitchen to the living area. Perhaps you'll spend a few minutes discussing your prospect's furnishings, and how he or she might arrange the room. Then let's say there's a fireplace. Ask your prospect to kneel down alongside you in front of it. Have them slide open the screen so you can demonstrate how the fireplace works. Instruct them in what to do, but let *them* do it. Explain how the vents above and below the firebox help to circulate warm air throughout the room. Let them operate the controls. Give them the chance to discover the benefits for themselves, through involvement. After all, it's going to be *their* home.

Minor orders help you dramatize by allowing you to demonstrate benefits, rather than show features. They also get people accustomed to doing the things we suggest. When people recognize that there are benefits behind everything we ask them to do, they'll trust us more. And trust, as all of us know, rests at the heart of every successful leasing effort.

Highlight relevant amenities. One of the biggest advantages to apartment living are the lifestyle amenities that many residents love to have at their fingertips. Round the clock access to tanning and exercise facilities. Lavish club-houses, available by reservation for meetings or parties. Luxurious indoor and outdoor pools, spas, and saunas. Racquetball, basketball, and tennis courts. Valet services like dry-cleaning pickup/delivery and restaurant reservations. The list keeps growing every day.

Depending on the amenities you offer, highlight the benefits you believe are *most likely* to interest your prospect. Remember this rule of thumb: If they don't care about it, don't sell it. In addition, maintain a relaxed pace during the amenities demonstration. You may have been through your facilities a thousand times, but remember that your prospect has not. Relate stories about memorable resident activities, or flip through some pictures of recent community events. And as always, keep looking for opportunities to get people involved.

Even if people never take advantage of amenities or participate in activities, most take comfort in knowing that they could if they wanted to. Amenities can add tremendous perceived value to an apartment in the minds of your future residents. Therefore, do your best to demonstrate the amenities you offer with enthusiasm, and with the prospect's individual preferences in mind.

SETTING THE STAGE FOR SUCCESS

The process of encouraging your prospect to participate in the demonstration strengthens the bonds of trust. You start encouraging involvement by giving minor orders. Each minor order invites a response. If your order is clearly intended to help the prospect discover a benefit, then your prospect's response will more than likely be cooperative. With each instance of cooperation, you build more trust, and when trust is built, commitment is much more likely to follow.

All of this sets the stage for what may be the most exciting step of all: inviting your prospect to lease. And even though there's a possibility your prospect may raise objections (which is an issue the next secret discusses in great detail) your chances for gaining a commitment increase when your demonstration offers more opportunities for involvement.

REVIEW

In this secret, we examined a number of strategies that will help us make effective and memorable demonstrations.

- Assemble a community information notebook, and carry it with you each time you demonstrate an apartment. Create sections labeled *Community Maps, Apartment Specifications, Neighborhood Information*, information *For New Residents*, and *Comparables*. Strive for quality and readability throughout.
- Study your competitors thoroughly and regularly.
- Before opening your leasing office, inspect the routes to model and target vacant apartments for things that might "turn off" future residents.

- Next, conduct detailed inspections of all vacant and furnished model interiors. Make absolutely certain that the apartments you intend to show are market-ready—*completely ready for occupancy*.
- Creatively accessorize market-ready apartments. The more fun you and your prospect have in the demonstration, the more likely they'll be to remember your apartment over others.
- Finally, make sure you're carrying keys that work.

As you finish the leasing interview and leave the office:

- Offer your prospect a choice of apartments to see.
- Make personal safety a priority.
- Keep the dialogue moving. Initiate conversation with open-ended questions, and remember the importance of honesty.
- Stay in step. Remain near to your prospect so that trust can continue to build.
- Unless low vacancy prevents you from doing otherwise, demonstrate vacant apartments before showing models.

Create a meaningful, benefit-oriented opening line. Avoid obvious comments like, "This is our two bedroom, one bath. . . ."

Let the demonstration begin:

- Present apartment features in terms of their benefits to your prospect. People don't lease features, which are factual in nature. They lease *benefits*, which have emotional appeal.
- Put your prospect's preferences first. Create a vision that places their stuff and their ideas in the spotlight.
- Get your prospect involved by giving them "minor orders." Minor orders help people discover benefits on their own and establish the foundation for gaining a financial commitment.
- Make sure that the orders you give will result in the discovery of key benefits to your prospect. Don't ask people to do things merely for the sake of doing them.
- When demonstrating lifestyle amenities (pool, exercise facilities, etc.) highlight the ones you feel are most likely to interest your prospect. Remember this rule of thumb: If they don't care about it, don't sell it.

Secret Number 4

- Getting your prospects involved in the demonstration sets the stage for success. If they cooperate with your minor orders along each step of the way, inviting them to lease will be a comfortable and natural thing to do.

Secret Number 5

Overcoming Objections Doesn't Work–Resolving Them Does

You gain strength, courage, and confidence with every experience that makes you stop and look fear in the face. . . . You must do the things you think you cannot do.

Eleanor Roosevelt

If there's one thing that has the power to strike dread and anxiety into the hearts of leasing professionals, it is that moment when a prospect objects. It doesn't matter how strong a person you may be: Facing objections can be scary. And not *just* for the salesperson. Salespeople fear objections for fear of losing the sale. That much is obvious. But prospects have their fears, too. They're afraid that if they object, the salesperson will assault them with a hailstorm of high pressure. Others are simply afraid of hurting a nice salesperson's feelings.

We become better able to manage the anxious energy caused by objections when we arrive at a deeper understanding of why and how people

object. In order for us to achieve that goal, we must first expose a serious flaw in our industry's perspective concerning this issue. It has to do with the traditional idea of "overcoming" objections.

WHY OVERCOMING OBJECTIONS DOESN'T WORK

You may think this sounds crazy, but overcoming objections does not work. For years, apartment leasing professionals have been trained to overcome or handle objections. What's more, we've frequently been told that unless we can overcome our prospect's objections, our chances of getting the deposit are slim. Well that, my friends, is dead wrong. In fact, from the standpoint of building positive customer relationships, nothing could be further from the truth.

Let's say I'm the leasing consultant showing you an apartment. I've been rigorously trained to overcome any conceivable objection you might raise. Let's say I'm so determined to overcome your objection that you don't stand a chance:

You: I don't like the color of the carpet.

Me: What do you mean you don't like the color of the carpet? It's the most versatile color you'll find anywhere, and because it's stain-resistant you won't have to worry so much about spills and dirt. (Then, with a note of finality, I say) Actually, this carpet is only a year old, and the owner says I can't replace it.

You: But I don't like the color.

Me: Look—carpet is carpet. Wherever you go, apartments use the same basic colors and the same basic quality. That's just the way things are. And once you get your furniture moved in, most of it gets covered up anyway. Here's what you do: Buy some throw rugs. You can put one here, and one there, and one down the center of the hallway. That will give it some more color, if color is what you're after. Besides, it's really not that bad. I've definitely seen worse.

You: Okay. Well . . . let me think it over, and I'll get back to you. (Exasperated, you leave.)

HA! Overcame your objection, didn't I? Steamrolled right over it. There was just one little problem: You went away without leaving a deposit. And you aren't likely to come back.

This is a prime example of how many salespeople are trained to overcome objections. And it really is too bad. A lot of great leasing opportunities are lost this way. Your dislike of the carpet color was only part of the reason you left. The main reason was that you didn't appreciate *being* overcome. That's why overcoming objections doesn't work.

Think about it. The word *overcome* speaks about power. It speaks about domination. To overcome means to conquer or defeat something—or in this case, *someone*. By its very definition, overcoming objections suggests that someone's going to get conquered. Someone's going to get defeated.

Most people, including those who are shopping for apartments, don't enjoy being defeated (especially when they are offering someone an opportunity to earn their business). If you approach objections from the standpoint of overcoming them, you may score a few points along the way, but in the end nobody will win. The prospect will simply tell you, "Let me think about it, and I'll call you tomorrow. . . ." which loosely translated means "You're a jerk, and I'm never coming back."

In the final analysis, as leasing professionals we will never win if we force our prospects to lose. If we are committed to working in the spirit of positive customer relations, we must accept nothing less than favorable outcomes for everybody involved. This is why, as an industry, it is so important that we stop using the phrase "overcoming objections." It is time to adopt a new perspective, one that enables us to demonstrate a higher degree of consideration to the customers we serve. Instead of overcoming our prospect's objections, we must learn to *resolve* them.

RESOLVING OBJECTIONS

The secret to alleviating a prospect's objections lies in *resolving* them. Resolving objections means exploring solutions to objections that are raised and working to settle them successfully. It means rationally examining concerns for the purpose of putting them to rest, not facing off to see which person's point of view will prevail.

When objecting prospects realize that instead of looking to win an argument you are trying to better understand their point of view, they are less likely to become defensive or unyielding. Rather, chances are better that they'll be more honest with their thoughts and more flexible toward the thing they are objecting to. You want them to know that unless everybody wins, nobody wins. And though you'll never resolve every objection you encounter, approaching objections from the standpoint of resolving them will help you respond to objections more positively—and move beyond them more predictably.

THE GOLDEN RULES OF RESOLVING OBJECTIONS

When it comes to resolving objections, there are two Golden Rules. The first is this:

Avoid Conflict.

Combatting objections in a direct frontal assault creates pressure, resentment, and hostility. In short, a head-on approach invites conflict. Take a moment to think of something in which you strongly believe a certain way. It could be anything (a spiritual law, a political cause, the way you load the dishwasher, or whatever). If a person aggressively challenges you for believing the way you do, how are you most likely to respond? Easy—chances are you will defend yourself. Even if you are obviously and absolutely wrong, that is what you are most likely to do.

The same thing can happen with your prospects. For example, debating a prospect over carpet color isn't likely to warm their heart. Instead, it is more likely to create friction and drive them away. So avoid conflict at all costs. It rarely, if ever, produces positive outcomes.

The second Golden Rule is this:

Seek Agreement.

As you've seen in previous sections, your prospect's point of view is really the only point of view that matters. Until they understand that

you're willing to see things from their point of view, they aren't likely to try seeing things from yours.

The beauty of seeking agreement with resistant prospects is that it helps cushion the manner in which you respond when they object. However, this is *not* to say that you should agree with your prospect's objections. Agreeing can be something as simple as nodding while your customer objects, and repeating their objection back so that they can see you're trying to understand, rather than challenge, their concern. The unspoken message you want to get across is, "Hey, I understand how you feel about this, and if I were you, chances are I'd feel the same way. What you're saying is important, and I'm listening to every word."

Objections simply cannot be resolved unless your prospect knows that you're willing to listen and understand, even if you don't completely agree with what is being said. Therefore, commit yourself to following the Golden Rules of resolving objections. In doing so, you'll develop the ability to resolve objections more comfortably than you ever thought possible.

WHAT CAUSES OBJECTIONS?

Before discussing what causes people to object, you need to recognize two very important truths about the whole issue of objections. Number one, people have the right to object. Prospects are free to say whatever they want about your apartments, regardless of whether we like what they say or not. If you don't acknowledge that right, you may get defensive, and defensive attitudes will destroy your leasing effectiveness. Besides, objections are rarely personal in nature. In most cases, objections are directed at structural or aesthetic aspects of an apartment or the community, and not at the leasing representative.

Number two, the line between objections and lies can be very, very fine. For instance, people may tell you they have "a few more places to look at," when in fact they've already looked at everything else in the area. For some apartment shoppers, lying to salespeople is perfectly legitimate behavior, because rather than viewing it as a sin, they regard it as a means of self-defense. If you plan to work in the apartment leasing business for long, you'll have to accept the fact that your prospects aren't always going to tell you the truth. No matter. It just means that sometimes you'll have to work a little harder to uncover and resolve the real issues.

Now let's move on. There are six common causes behind most of the objections we encounter in the apartment leasing business:

Procrastination

Procrastination is the shadowy culprit behind many of the objections we encounter in the leasing environment. While there are certainly countless reasons that people procrastinate, one is particularly common among apartment shoppers: The fear of making a bad decision. And who can blame them? In the Puget Sound region alone, there are approximately *400,000* apartments to choose from. With so many options, the chances of someone making the wrong choice and experiencing buyer's remorse is high. Therefore, rather than deal with what might be a difficult decision, many people simply refuse to take action, thinking it's the safest thing to do.

The only problem is, it isn't safe at all. Procrastination rarely pays. The following sign recently appeared in a community leasing office:

> The apartment you saw today
> and plan to lease tomorrow
> is the apartment someone else saw
> yesterday and plans to lease today

Procrastination is tough to contend with. It can have a paralyzing effect on apartment shoppers. They may even reach a point where they can't decide which would be worse—making a decision and regretting it, or not making a decision and suffering because of it.

Fear/Mistrust

These two closely related obstacles may be the greatest challenges we face. Many people enter leasing offices with suspicion and defensiveness as a result of having been deceived or mistreated in the past. They may dread being pressured into leasing an apartment they don't want. They may fear making a hasty decision they'll wind up regretting later. Or, they may have

trouble trusting people they know are compensated on the basis of whether or not a deal gets done. Even though a person's fear or mistrust may be completely unfounded, either or both often lurk behind many of the objections we face.

Price

The issue of price is a very interesting basis for objections. In cases where people object over price, they're usually experiencing anxiety on one of three fronts: (1) anxiety over whether or not they can actually afford the price; (2) anxiety over having the salesperson ram a justification for the price down their throats; and (3) anxiety over whether or not they are getting the best deal possible. Since people are sometimes unwilling to reveal their difficulty in coming to terms with the price, the price objection is often camouflaged by comments like, "I need to think it over," or "I'm just looking."

Price objections are also used to mask other, more specific objections. For example, when a prospect says, "It's too expensive" there may be different issues at play that the prospect is reluctant to express. Sometimes even the most experienced eye can have trouble seeing what those issues really are.

Third-Party Approval

It is frustrating to give a flawless and enthusiastic demonstration, only to find that a prospect can't commit without the consent of someone else. Oftentimes, people will present themselves as the main decision maker, when in actuality they are pre-screening apartments for themselves and their spouse or roommate. As the "designated shopper," they want all the information they can get, and in order to get it they need to draw you into a full-blown demonstration—even though they have no intention of making an immediate commitment.

Uncertainty/Confusion

Let's face it—people shopping for apartments have a tendency to get confused. After a full day of apartment shopping, things start looking and sounding the same. Brochures cover the dashboard or coffee table. Rental magazines stack up. Prospects become unsure about which of the floorplans they've seen is best-suited to what they need. They may not be certain which geographic location is the most convenient. Uncertainty and confusion can be very real issues in an apartment shopper's life, especially in large metropolitan areas with massive concentrations of apartments.

Courtesy

Certain forms of objections result from a desire to be courteous in all circumstances. Some people have a hard time being honest about their dislikes, especially if they think that by expressing them they'll hurt someone's feelings. Others avoid confrontation at all costs. They don't want to upset someone's day by coming right out and expressing disapproval about something they don't like. Still others simply have a hard time saying no to gracious, helpful people.

Finally, some people don't like drawing attention to themselves. They don't want to make a scene. They lead quiet, undisturbed lives and prefer to keep things that way—even if it means not resolving issues as important as finding a home. As a result, their objections can be mysterious and difficult to identify.

DIFFERENT FORMS OF OBJECTIONS

Many leasing professionals don't realize that objections take on two distinctly different forms. One is known as the *deflection*. The other is known as the *true objection*. First we'll look at deflections—what they are, how you can recognize them, and some ways that you can successfully resolve them. Next, we'll examine true objections, looking first at some examples, and then discussing several techniques for confidently resolving many of the ones we frequently encounter.

Deflections

Without a doubt, some of the most frustrating obstacles encountered in apartment leasing are known as *deflections*. Deflections are vague or evasive statements people make to conceal their real thoughts or feelings.

Here are some of the more common deflections:

"It's too expensive."
"I need to think about it."
"I'm just looking/I have a few more places to look at."
"I just want a brochure and some prices."
"I'm not going to decide today (need for the future)."
"I need to come back with my spouse/roommate."
"I'll take an application and bring it back."

In the following section we are going to examine each of these deflections one by one, focusing first on the underlying causes behind them. Then, we'll explore some solutions that can help you resolve them and keep you moving in the direction of securing a commitment from your prospect.

"It's too expensive." While there will always be individuals for whom this statement is true, the too-expensive deflection is more often used as a cloaking device for other objectionable issues in the prospect's mind. In fact, it may be the apartment shopper's deflection of choice. The reason is this: Personal finances are usually a confidential matter, and many prospects know that many salespeople are hesitant to press for information along confidential lines. In short, a large percentage of consumers recognize that the too-expensive deflection is a subtle, yet effective, way to give salespeople the brush.

If it becomes apparent that your rent is clearly more than your prospect can afford, do what is best for both parties. Refer them to another community if you can and move on to your next prospect. However, in cases where you believe that people are merely using "too expensive" to deflect you, understand first that it may be the result of inaccurate comparisons between your rents and (1) the rent your prospect is currently paying; or (2) the rent being charged at competing communities.

Always make sure that apples are being compared with apples. If you find that your prospect is comparing your rent to what they are paying now, or to competitors down the street, find out what those communities include with their price. Chances are, if your rents are higher, those buildings offer less in some way than yours does. And if the physical or geographical differences are small, remember this: People lease *service* every bit as much as they lease the apartments themselves. Much of the reason a person is going to lease from you will come down to the impression you make in their minds. Recognize that *you* add value to the price as well.

In addition, those using the too-expensive deflection may not be aware of other financial benefits—known as *compensating factors*—that might actually help to *save* a person money by reducing monthly expenses for childcare, commuting, utilities, parking, storage, health club dues, and the like. If this is the case, make sure you sit down together and list which compensating factors might help make up the difference between your rents and their pocketbook.

When faced with people asserting that your rents are too high, simply respond with some diplomatic open-ended questions:

***"Why** do you feel that we're too expensive?"*

***"What** are you comparing our prices to?"*

*"By living at our community, **how** do you think you might actually save money over where you live now, or other places you've looked?"*

Be patient and respectful when asking these questions. Remember, people can be very sensitive when it comes to discussing finances. Nevertheless, ask. It's your right. Stand your ground and wait for an answer. Your prospect's response may reveal an issue other than price, or it may reveal additional information to help you better understand their concerns. Regardless of how your prospect responds, you'll know that you've done your best to validate your price, stand behind your company, and demonstrate your commitment to do what it takes. Nobody can ask you for more than that.

One last note on price deflections. Even though the temptation may be strong, never debate a prospect on the issue of price. You'll almost always lose.

"I need to think about it." This vague deflection is also used to camouflage other, more specific objections. While apartment shoppers often *do* need time to weigh the consequences of their decisions, the "think about it" deflection usually results in a lose-lose situation for everyone involved.

Here's why. If a prospect is just procrastinating, or is not being honest about what's really on their mind, they may be unwittingly

walking away from the best option available to them. We see this almost daily in prospects who leave to "think about it," then frantically come rushing back with checkbooks in hand to discover that "their" apartment was leased to someone else. What's every bit as aggravating in these cases is that we've been denied the opportunity to render the professional services we're trained and paid to provide. The prospect isn't giving him or herself a fair opportunity to decide, and they're not giving us a fair opportunity to serve their needs.

One tactful approach to resolving the "think about it" deflection is the following series of three questions, tailored especially to help you clear away smokescreens and expose *exactly* what it is that people want to think about. It involves using a subtle process of elimination to get at the real issues. Here's how a conversation incorporating these questions might go:

Prospect: I need to think about it.
You: (nodding in agreement) I understand . . . and you should. You're making a big decision. But tell me—is it something about my company that concerns you?
Prospect: (more than likely will say) No.
You: Then is there something I've done or said to offend you?
Prospect: (again, more than likely will say) Of course not!
You: (with genuine sincerity) Then what is it? Is it [the suspected objection]?

In short, courage and determination are the keys to successfully resolving "think about it" deflections. In the words of Eleanor Roosevelt, " . . .You must do the things you think you cannot do." And remember, it is our responsibility to help tentative people make good decisions. Don't just let them walk away to "think about it" without searching for the deeper issues at play. If you create the opportunity for people to follow your lead, more of them will. And you'll be rewarded for it.

"I'm just looking/I have a few more places to look at." People are free to go wherever they want to go, and look wherever they want to look. Trying to dissuade someone from looking at competitors' apartments in your area will backfire more often than it will succeed. That is why it is

more effective to ask the just-looking prospect what else they've seen and where else they're planning to visit.

Before doing that, though, it is important to again address the issue of what to say about competitors when presented with the opportunity. While no one ever said we have to be best buddies with the competition, in an industry as close-knit as ours it is important that we regard them with objectivity and respect.

Of course, this can be easier said than done. When a prospect mentions a competitor that they're shopping besides you, the temptation to knock that competitor down a few pegs can suddenly become tough to resist, especially if you know they run a lousy operation. However, you *must not* sink to the level of criticizing or condemning your competitors. Prospects quickly recognize mudslinging. Many people's sense of fair play is offended by it, mainly because the party under attack isn't present to defend themselves. Even if what you say is undeniably true, there's a strong possibility that it will make you look bad. People who sling mud usually can't avoid getting some on themselves.

In addition, leasing professionals who put down competitors also run a very high risk of unknowingly insulting their prospects. Badmouthing other communities your prospect may have visited creates a subtle implication that because they chose to look at an "inferior" apartment, they exercised inferior judgment.

So what is the most ethical approach to take? First, gather as many specific details about your competitors' apartments as you possibly can (using a comparable market survey worksheet like the one in Secret Number 4). Research their floorplan types, their floorplan distribution (number of studio, one, two, and three bedrooms), rents and deposits, current concessions, amenities, special services, key policies, and their community density (measured in apartments per acre; generally speaking, 10 or less is considered low density, 10 to 20 is considered medium, and over 20 is considered high). Then list and highlight the strengths of your apartments and community that give you the advantage.

Keep these comparisons in your community information notebook, and remember: If you actually choose to show this information to your

prospect, verbalize only *your* strengths. *Do not speak what you feel are your competitors' weaknesses!* In categories where you beat the competition, call attention only to your facts. For example,

> *"Our apartments were designed without fireplaces, which is a terrific benefit. That fact alone increases the total available living and storage space in this apartment by almost 80 cubic feet."*

Then, once you've presented your strengths, buckle down and bite your tongue. Let your prospect draw their own comparisons. When given the chance, it is remarkable what people are capable of figuring out on their own.

Sometimes, however, prospects will start fishing around for dirt, like why a competitor's rents are lower or why they're offering move-in specials. Here's a word to the wise: Be careful. Though the bait is tempting, don't take it. Instead, stick to the facts. Do *not* speculate or offer opinions about your competitors. If other people have started rumors or gossip, take it upon yourself to stop them. Maintain neutrality, so that your prospects can draw their own conclusions. Remain completely objective and professional. Concentrate only on building your prospect's confidence in *you*, and the apartment you represent. Earn their business fair and square. That is the standard of integrity for which we all must strive.

Now—back to the just-looking deflection. If a prospect says they are just looking, encourage them to describe the different places they've seen, and the other places they intend to visit. Use variations of the second Magic Question (**please tell me about**):

> *"What can you tell me about the other places you've seen?"*
> *"Would you mind telling me about the apartment you saw over at The Lakes?"*

or,

> *"Tell me about some of the other places you plan to visit."*

If you can, get them to specifically describe what they are looking for; perhaps all you need to do is direct their attention to something both of you simply overlooked. If the communities they mention are your competitors', get busy and refer to your community information notebook. And if you decide to show the actual information to your prospect, remember: Stick to the facts. Let them draw their own conclusions.

For the person who is "just looking," time inevitably becomes a pressing factor. There aren't many people who shop for apartments because they have nothing better to do with their spare time. Therefore, instead of letting people who are just looking simply walk out the door, use the information at your disposal to help them *save time*. If you do that, especially for people who have reached the point of exasperation in their apartment search, you'll find many more people placing their trust—and their rental dollars—with you.

"I just want a brochure and some prices." Prospects who use this deflection are often in a hurry. They leave their car idling out front, rush in, and breathlessly ask for a brochure with some prices. Then they rush back out.

However, this is also a typical way for some people to shop for apartments. Instead of using the phone to make their preliminary selections or submitting to actual apartment demonstrations, they simply drive around and gather information first. Whichever is the case, the best way to resolve this deflection is to *slow your prospect down*.

An excellent way to accomplish this is to ask a Magic Question:

> *"I can appreciate that you're in a hurry, and I promise not to take up much of your time, but I'm just curious: Could you take just a couple of moments and describe for me the things you're looking for in a new apartment?"*

or,

> *"I know you don't have much time, but what can you tell me about where you're living now?"*

Many times, people aren't as busy as they think they are. In addition, most people have uncanny ways of *finding* time to talk about themselves. When next you encounter a person who "just wants the facts," try to get them talking. While watching closely for signs of impatience, get as much information as their time will permit. Obviously you don't want to aggravate people by causing them delay, but as always, the more information you get, the better your chances of leasing another apartment will become.

"I'm not going to decide today (need for the future)." Even though many apartment shoppers do indeed begin their apartment search 60 days or more in advance of their move, "future" is a very common deflection.

Many people saying they need something in the future are merely procrastinating. If that is the case, all it may take is some reassurance that making a commitment *today* would be doing the right thing. First, make your best effort to determine how soon they need an apartment. Summarize and highlight the benefits you offer that fit your prospect's needs, and point out that everything can be theirs *right now*, unless there's a legitimate and compelling reason for them to postpone their decision. If someone truly needs to decide, there is no advantage to be gained by waiting. More time rarely results in better decisions. *More information*, however, usually does.

Provided it is legal and in line with your company's policies, you might also try offering to "hold" an apartment for a certain time period with a downpayment on the security deposit. This is often a very effective method, as it gives the future prospect the best of both worlds—an apartment, plus an escape route if they change their minds. If your prospect agrees to place a "hold deposit," congratulate them on their decision. Then encourage them to relax. Doing so subtly discourages any further looking on their part and decreases the odds that they'll bail out. (See Secret Number 6 for more information on the "Temporary Hold.")

Finally, if you sense that a person is using the "won't decide today/future" deflection because they are wary of you, don't try compensating for it by shifting into sales overdrive. Ease off. Better yet, use a softer approach. Say "You know, maybe you *should* take some time to make sure this is what you want." Your prospect won't have been expecting you

to agree. Now all of a sudden they realize that you're not looking at them as a dollar sign. Their levels of comfort and trust will rise. Then, when you recommend that they put down money to hold an apartment, they'll be more likely to act on your advice.

"I need to come back with my spouse/roommate." Again, the reasons behind this deflection can vary. Because some prospects do the preliminary shopping for both themselves and another person, they will masquerade as the primary decision maker to ensure that they're given as much information as possible. In other cases, fear or mistrust are behind this deflection. It can also be a lie.

The most sensible approach to resolving "I need to come back" is prevention. Here is a question that should be asked early in every telephone presentation you make and with every walk-in prospect you greet: "Will you be making this decision yourself, or will you be making it together with someone else?" If a prospect calling on the phone indicates that there will indeed be someone else involved, schedule the appointment so that all necessary parties can be present. If a new prospect walks into your office and you receive the same reply, *pour everything you've got into your demonstration*. Find out the name of the third party, and include them in the process by referring to them often in your conversation. Concentrate on building the first person's enthusiasm for the apartment as high as possible. Once that has been accomplished, they'll become your strongest ally with the other. Then, when everyone involved is finally present, many times all you'll have to do is stand back and watch your ally lease the apartment for you.

Here's one more idea. If person #1 likes an apartment, but deflects you by saying they'll have to come back with person #2, do this: Encourage them to place a temporary hold on the apartment. Guarantee a full refund within 24 hours if person #2 sees the apartment and disapproves. Emphasize to #1 that the only thing worse than #2 not liking the apartment would be if #2 *did* like it, but it had been leased to someone else. Based on that consideration, encourage #1 to make a decision. Make it clear that they simply cannot lose.

"I'll take an application and bring it back." When prospects say this, you've usually gained their trust, but there are probably still issues that

have yet to be resolved in their minds. These people *want* to lease an apartment; otherwise, they wouldn't have asked for an application.

Though it is true that prospects have been known to take applications and bring them back with deposit checks in hand; as a general rule, it is poor leasing form to follow along with this ploy. More often than not, the be-back routine is nothing more than a deflection borne out of courtesy that prospects use to make an escape while letting us save face.

For heaven's sake, don't just let people who are obviously interested get into their cars and drive away. Instead, when next you have a person who just wants to take an application and leave, try responding like this: "I'm getting the impression that you're still unsettled about something, but I'm not sure what it is. Is there an area I haven't covered well enough, or was it something I said?" At this point, most people will open up with more information; they don't want you thinking you did something wrong when you didn't. Their response may provide the missing piece of the puzzle—one you never would have found without trying just a little bit harder.

A secret strategy for resolving deflections. One of the most powerful secrets to resolving deflections is that they can often be neutralized before they're ever brought up. Here's how you can do it: Before you even begin discussing specifics in your leasing interview, make a statement like this:

> *"Nobody's going to try selling you anything you don't want. I'm just going to show you some of the things people like best about living here. All you need to do is take an open, honest look at what we have to offer, and decide whether or not it fits what you're looking for. Fair enough?"*

It is remarkable how a comment like this can disarm defensive or evasive prospects. It is so reasonable, so confident, and so democratic that people suddenly find themselves unwilling to jerk you around. As with many of the other relationship selling techniques you've seen in this book, it shows that when you build trust, the walls of resistance and defense come tumbling down.

True Objections

The second form of objection we encounter in apartment leasing is known as the *true objection*. Whereas deflections are often vague and evasive, true objections are typically much more tangible and specific in nature.

True objections can be raised in relation to a wide variety of apartment and community characteristics. Here are a number to which people frequently object, in no particular order:

- Availability
- Carpet color/quality
- Laundry features
- Price
- Amenities (or lack of)
- Traffic noise
- Storage
- Room size
- Interior light (or lack of)
- Quality/condition/cleanliness of apartment interiors
- Location (ground/middle/top)
- Appliances
- Lease terms
- Parking
- Neighborhood reputation
- Pet policies
- Property appearance
- Absence of a move-in special (especially when competitors are offering them)

Resolving true objections. We face an amazing array of true objections in the apartment leasing business. "These appliances are too old. I need a washer and dryer. The bedrooms are too small. I can hear traffic noise. I don't want a ground floor. You don't have covered parking. I can't stand beige carpeting. This apartment is too dark. You don't have an exercise room. The closets aren't big enough." And on and on and on.

There are two very important points to recognize about true objections. First, true objections are something you should welcome. It may sound weird, but if prospects weren't genuinely interested, *they would not object*. They would just evade you with deflections until they could get away. An objecting prospect is a person who has reached a point where *almost* everything is okay—a little more information and a little more reassurance is usually all that's needed before putting down a deposit feels like the right thing for them to do.

The second point is that you must never ignore objections. For that

matter, you shouldn't even hesitate in responding to them. If you remain silent or hesitate when a prospect objects, they're likely to think that (1) you're no more certain about the value of your product than they are, or (2) you're not being sensitive to their concern. Neither should you ignore obvious negatives, like jet aircraft noise or dark lighting. If obviously unappealing things are not acknowledged, prospects are very liable to assume that the leasing person is trying to gloss them over. The only way to keep your credibility from being instantly destroyed is to acknowledge the obvious, without making it a major issue. Present it in as positive a manner as you can, and then proceed with enthusiasm.

Unless you respond to objections or negatives quickly and with confidence, your leasing effectiveness can be diminished. That's why it is so important that you prepare yourself in advance for the objections you know you're bound to face. In the following section, we'll look at three different approaches that you can use, starting today, to more consistently resolve true objections with confidence and grace.

One step ahead. This is one of the most effective, and underused, methods of dealing with true objections that there is. Not only is it proactive, but it's preventative; and when dealing with true objections an ounce of calculated prevention can be worth many pounds of cure.

A good example of this technique appears in Secret Number 1, where the true objection concerning apartments without washers and dryers was addressed. Let's select another tough objection from our list—traffic noise—and look again at an example of how staying one step ahead of true objections really works.

Though there are things we can do in vacant apartments to help compensate for traffic noise (i.e., small radios, fans, etc.), it is usually an issue over which we have little control. Before your prospect even has a chance to comment on audible traffic noise in the apartment, you might say something like this: "It's interesting when you think about the sounds in this apartment. . . . sometimes people worry that sounds from the outside will be disturbing and unpleasant, and that's definitely understandable. However, this is a completely vacant apartment. Any sound seems amplified in an empty space like this. Even our own voices seem a little louder, don't you think?

"That's what makes it so interesting. These six-inch exterior walls absorb a tremendous amount of the sound from outside. So do the insulated glass windows. After you fill the room with furniture, a lot of sound will be absorbed. Then, once you're living here, even more will be masked over by your television, appliances, stereo, hairdryer, plumbing, and so forth. Of course, you may notice some sound getting ready for work in the morning or coming home at night, but that's when the streets are busiest. Between 10:00 p.m. and 6:00 a.m., things really quiet down."

You might close by saying this: "I'll be completely honest with you—it's something you may be aware of for a week or two. But after that, people typically notice it less and less. In fact, most people eventually reach the point where they rarely, if ever, even notice it at all."

Staying one step ahead of objectionable issues is particularly effective; it allows you to subtly agree with your prospect on one hand, while demonstrating your honesty, integrity, and problem-solving abilities on the other. If you wait for prospects to raise objections about obviously objectionable things, you relinquish an important advantage. You also lose credibility if you intentionally ignore negatives that are plain to see. So take the initiative. Stay one step ahead of true objections. Raise them yourself, and then present the best possible solutions in confident, customer-oriented terms. By doing so, you can prevent tough objections from derailing the momentum of your demonstrations.

The feel/felt/found technique. In his 1984 book entitled *The Best Seller*, sales trainer Ron Willingham outlined a technique that revolutionized the way salespeople in many professions respond to (and resolve) tough objections. It's known as the *feel/felt/found* technique, and it is remarkably effective in helping resolve many of the tougher objections we face when leasing apartments.

Here's how it works. When a prospect objects to something, first acknowledge their concern by expressing that understand how they must *feel*. Then, you point out that others who have leased at your community once *felt* the same way as your prospect does now. Finally, much like relating a testimonial from a satisfied customer, reveal what other people eventually *found* that helped them overcome their concerns and decide to move in. It's simple, flexible, and effective. *Feel, felt, found.*

Used with tact and grace, *feel/felt/found* works to reassure your prospects that you have no intention of debating them over the concern they've raised. It also allows you to demonstrate that having concerns is natural and okay. Furthermore, it does wonders to help defuse confrontational issues. Let's say a prospect suddenly objects to the fact that you don't have a clubhouse equipped with swimming pool and fitness-related amenities. Here's how you might respond, using *feel/felt/found*:

> *"You know, I can appreciate how you* ***feel*** *about wanting a place to exercise, because I understand how important health and fitness are to you. Interestingly enough, a number of other people living here once* ***felt*** *the same way you do right now.*
>
> *"However, after looking around the area, they* ***found*** *that our rents are considerably lower than communities who have to pass the costs of equipping and maintaining clubhouse facilities on to their residents. In fact, a number of our residents have taken the dollars they save living here and joined XYZ Athletics down the street. At XYZ, they get a bigger and better quality selection of equipment—not to mention free service from the club's personal fitness consultants. There isn't an apartment community in town with facilities better than XYZ's. And as an added plus, XYZ gives our residents 20 percent off on new memberships. Is that something you think might work?"*

You can use *feel/felt/found* in almost any situation that involves a true objection. Not only does it enable you to meet tough objections with confidence, but it allows you to do so in a diplomatic and considerate manner.

A final word of advice on *feel/felt/found*—before using it in a real leasing situation, take the time to prepare. Start by listing your toughest objections on paper. Next, write out *feel/felt/found* solutions for each. Once that's complete, practice the responses you develop by role playing with a co-worker, spouse, or trusted friend. Then, put them into action in your leasing presentations. Take a moment and refer back to the Golden Rules of resolving objections (on pages 98 and 99). When you do, you'll see that *feel/felt/found* makes following those rules a whole lot easier.

Two options. In addition to staying one step ahead and using feel/felt/found, we can also offer prospects two options for resolving an objection they've expressed. There's something about being offered a choice that helps people feel less pressured, and more a part of having contributed to the final solution. And in case you are wondering, there is a reason for using two: It's important to keep things under control. Offer more than two and you may wind up with a wild goose chase on your hands.

To illustrate this technique, let's take on an issue that generates scores of objections: carpet. Objections over carpet never seem to end. People think it's too old, or the wrong color, or the seams are too obvious, or it's faded, or it has stains, tears, or burn marks—you name it. Obviously, if a carpet is completely trashed it should be replaced. But if people are just being picky, there is still hope. You can try resolving the issue by giving them a couple of reasonable options to choose from. Here's how you might respond:

> *"I can appreciate your concerns about the carpet, and if I were you, chances are I'd feel the same. But since this apartment works for you in pretty much every other way, let's take a look at our options.*
>
> *"We basically have two options. Number one, we can replace the carpet. If we replace it, you'll pay a slightly higher price, but then you'll have exactly what you want. Number two, we can leave it the way it is. If we leave it like it is, not only will you save money, but I can show you some great ideas for using throw rugs or runners in the areas you're concerned about.*
>
> *"So you see, we have a couple of different options to choose from. Which of the two do you think might work best?"*

Here is a point you do not want to miss: If instead of presenting two options we'd have responded by saying, "Sorry—the owner said I can't replace this carpet," our prospect would probably have walked out. Even if what the owner had said was true, all our prospect would have heard is, "Sorry pal. I don't make the rules. Take it or leave it."

Our industry has enough trouble with being viewed by the public as inflexible. We don't want to make matters worse. A "one policy fits all" attitude is absolute suicide when attempting to resolve serious objections. Let's try to be more *flexible* with our prospects, even if the rules are tight. Preparing options in advance of the true objections we face will show people we're committed to finding solutions that make sense for each unique individual. To the extent that we're willing to work with our future residents, they'll be more willing to work with us.

COMPETING WITH MOVE-IN SPECIALS

One of the toughest challenges you will ever encounter in the leasing office is when a prospect says, "I can get the exact same apartment down the street. The only difference is *they'll* give me a full month's free rent." Here's the secret to succeeding in this difficult circumstance: Never base your response on price. Base it instead on *value*.

Unfortunately, the two most common methods of competing with move-in specials do not focus on value. As a result, neither is very effective. The first is where the leasing consultant announces to the prospect without explanation that, "*We* don't *need* to offer specials." The second is where the leasing consultant's goal is to plant a seed of doubt in the mind of the prospect with a comment like, "Whenever the other guys offer free rent, there's *always a reason. . . .*"

The first is arrogant. The second is spiteful. Neither promotes goodwill nor reflects integrity on the part of the person saying them. As an industry, we must hold to a higher standard. We must believe in our hearts that the value we offer—in our apartments, in our communities, and in our personal commitment to serving the customer—is fairly priced.

Remember this: If high quality and reliable service are the things an apartment shopper cares about most, they simply can't be had at the lowest price. Period. Companies that market high-quality products and offer exceptional customer service simply do not offer the lowest prices. Think about it. If all anybody ever wanted was low prices, no one would drive Cadillacs or BMWs. And companies like Nordstrom would be out of business.

If the apartments you offer and the services you render are outstanding, there is absolutely no reason whatsoever to apologize for the prices you ask. You have every right to be *fiercely proud* of your prices and the value they represent. You must let that pride shine, in everything you say and do. If you don't believe in the value of the prices you're asking, neither will your prospects.

Therefore, the surest way to lease apartments in the face of concessions is to enthusiastically present the apartment you offer in terms of the *value it represents* for your customer's leasing dollar. No, your rents may not be the lowest. And no, you may not be offering a special. You must become convinced within yourself that your apartments, and the service you provide, would be a bargain at any price. The most important sale you ever make will take place on the day you yourself become sold on the product you're selling.

So next time you're working with a prospect who is being enticed by a competitor's move-in specials, take heart and respond with something like this:

> *"You know, I'm glad you brought that up. And I can appreciate how you* ***feel*** *about their offer. In fact, a number of our most satisfied residents* ***felt*** *the same way you do before they moved in. But then they realized something. They* ***found*** *that we offer the two things people want most in a home: exceptional quality and exceptional service. However, high quality and premium service cannot be had at the lowest price. Since I know that quality and service are as important to you as they are to the rest of our residents, I'm certain you'll find your experience with us to be worth every penny—and then some. Why don't you give us a try?"*

Champions in our industry don't retreat in the face of deflections. Nor do they back down and surrender in the face of true objections. They don't seek to advance their position by slinging mud at others. And they don't cave in when challenged by competitor giveaways. Instead, they

strive to increase their occupancies by working with their prospective residents in a spirit of cooperation and mutual respect. They unflinchingly demonstrate a wholehearted belief in the *value* their apartments represent. In short, they walk with their heads held high.

And theirs is the example we should all try to follow. Though resolving objections can be unnerving and tough, achieving success in the face of adversity is what builds our character and makes us strong.

REVIEW

- *Overcoming* objections doesn't work. Instead, you must strive for favorable outcomes by *resolving* the objections you encounter.
- The Golden Rules of Resolving Objections are to *avoid conflict* and to *seek agreement*.
- There are six common causes behind most of the objections you face:

Procrastination	Price	Third-Party Approval
Fear/Mistrust	Courtesy	Uncertainty/Confusion

- There are two different forms of objections:

  Deflections, which are vague comments people use either to evade you or to mask their true objections, and

  True objections, which are more specific and can relate to a variety of things, including carpet color/quality, room size, parking, and so forth.

- Deflections are best resolved through patient, assertive questioning.
- True objections can be resolved through use of the following techniques:

  One Step Ahead
  Feel/Felt/Found
  Two Options

- When competing with concessions, boldly present what you have to offer in terms of the *value it represents* for your customer's leasing dollar. Many prospects will lease first-rate quality and exceptional service before they'll chase after a low price.

Secret Number 6

Invite Your Prospects To Lease

There is only one way to get anybody to do anything . . . and that is by making the other person want to do it. There simply is no other way.

Dale Carnegie

You have now arrived at one of the most exciting (and arguably most important) stages in the apartment leasing process: That moment when you invite your prospect to lease. It is a moment of great significance, considering all the effort required to make it possible. First there was a top-notch telephone presentation, which resulted in a warm and friendly greeting. The greeting was soon followed by a comfortable, mutually informative leasing interview. Then an apartment was demonstrated, and a variety of objections were resolved to the prospect's satisfaction. In short, a relationship was built, and when you think about it, good relationship building involves a considerable amount of work.

However, something often occurs that takes all that work and throws it out the window. Or to be more precise, something *does not* occur. In many cases, the leasing representative completes every step

of the leasing process except one. They never invite their prospect to lease.

This is perhaps one of the greatest tragedies of the apartment management profession. Every day across America, thousands of prospective residents walk away from apartments for a very simple reason. The reason is not because they don't want to lease. The real reason is because *no one invites them* to lease. And what a shame. Think of the advertising dollars gone to waste. Think of the money that property owners will continue to lose through vacancy loss. Worst of all, think of the people who needed someone's assistance in finding a new home—and didn't get it.

As long as people meet your leasing criteria for rental history, creditworthiness, and employment/income, you must invite them to lease. Put another way, *every qualified prospect must get an invitation*. If someone walks away from your community without leasing, it should never be said that it was because no one asked them to.

This secret you are about to read is devoted to raising your awareness of the critical importance of inviting your prospects to lease. There is far too much at stake to do otherwise. But before looking at strategies for how you can improve your closing ratios, we are first going to examine some of the industry's oldest closing techniques in action. The reason? Part of knowing what to do is knowing what *not* to do. Once again, here's Lisa to demonstrate just a few of these approaches in another conversation with Bill:

Lisa: Bill, won't it be nice to relax on your terrace after a long day at work? (Trial Close)

Bill: I guess.

Lisa: Then let's just go ahead and get your paperwork started, okay? (ABC Close)

Bill: I don't know if I'm ready for that yet.

Lisa: Oh come on—sure you are! You will enjoy having a washer and dryer right in your apartment, won't you Bill? (second Trial Close)

Bill: Yeah.

Lisa: All right then. When do you want to move into our community? (Assumptive Close)

Bill: I'm not really sure.

Lisa (cutting in): Doesn't matter—we'll be ready when you are. Your furniture will fit perfectly in here, don't you think? (third Trial Close)

Bill: I hadn't thought much about the furniture yet.

Lisa: Well whatever you do, don't wait. In fact, you'd better put down your deposit right now. This is the only one bedroom I have left, and if you don't lease it today someone else is gonna get it. (Urgency Close)

Bill: Well if that happens, it probably wasn't meant to be.

Lisa: Don't *let* it happen! Listen to me, Bill. Come on now. All I need is your Okay, Okay? (Gimmick: The Double-Okay Close.)

A CLOSER LOOK AT TRADITION

The methods we just saw Lisa demonstrate are *actual closing techniques* that have been widely promoted throughout the apartment industry. In fact, there's a good chance you may have recognized a few. Whether you did or did not, the point is this: As leasing professionals, it's time we take a closer look at how we've traditionally asked for our prospect's business. But why? What's wrong with the way things have always been done? In some cases, the answer is nothing. But in others, the answer is absolutely everything.

This next section addresses some of our industry's most time-honored closing strategies, and discusses the various advantages and drawbacks of each.

Trial Closing

The first traditional closing technique Lisa demonstrated in the previous scenario is known as the "trial close." Trial closing is a questioning process intended to help salespeople gauge when their prospect is ready to commit. The idea behind trial closing is to periodically ask questions that are likely to result in a "yes" response from the prospect: "Will your furniture fit in here?" is one example of a traditional trial closing question. According to the theory, the more often your prospect says yes in response to trial closing questions, the more likely they are to lease.

While it is indeed important to measure a prospect's level of interest at various points along the way, trial closing can badly offend those on the receiving end. Recently, an apartment industry training publication presented advice on trial closing. The article, which was erroneously entitled "*Trail* Close," recommended that leasing professionals ask questions like this: "Will you enjoy having . . . right in your apartment?" Another suggested "trail" closing question was this: "Won't it be nice to relax on your terrace after a long day at work?" It went on to say that the "trail" close could be used "over and over until the future resident *reacts properly*" (italics mine).

Wow. The entire piece was a classic example of how good ideas go bad. Think about this for a moment: If someone asked *you* such obviously transparent questions, would you know what was up? Chances are that you would. You'd probably be thinking to yourself, "This salesperson is just trying to get me to say yes." And you know what? You'd be right.

Here's another question: What do we call it when people use shrewd tactics to influence our thinking and try to make us "react properly"? You're right again—it's called *manipulation*. There is absolutely *no faster way* to create resentment and destroy leasing opportunities than to bait trusting prospects with blatantly manipulative questions.

However, this is not to say we should discard the trial closing process. In spite of the way it has been misused, trial closing still has great value in apartment leasing. Trial close questioning helps us gauge our prospect's interest throughout the leasing encounter. It enables us to determine what things people like. And it helps us pinpoint the things they don't. Most importantly, it makes knowing when to ask for a commitment possible. Later in this chapter, we will be looking at friendlier, more up-to-date methods of evaluating our prospect's readiness to lease (see "Measure Interest" further ahead).

ABC (Always Be Closing)

At a seminar very early in my leasing career, I was taught the "ABCs of Leasing." Perhaps you've heard of them, too. ABC is an acronym that stands for "always be closing" Its intended purpose is to get salespeople closing early and closing often.

I walked out of that seminar convinced I'd discovered the solution to my struggles with closing. It seemed pretty simple; I wasn't closing early enough, and I wasn't closing often enough. All I needed to do was "always be closing," and my leasing percentages would soar.

Instead, they sank like a brick. People retreated from me as if I had the plague. It didn't make sense; I'd been told that ABC was *the* secret to success in closing, but instead of leasing more apartments, I was leasing even less. What was happening?

Not long afterward, I attended another leasing seminar where the ABC concept surfaced again. There was a workbook that went along with the course, and among its questions in the section on closing were two that made matters even worse than before. The first question was, "What's the best time to close?" The answer was "*Anytime!*" Okay, I thought to myself. Been there. Done that.

Then, near the bottom of the very same page, another question asked, "What is the result of a mistimed sale?" Here was the answer: "*A lost sale, every time.*" Immediately I began to wonder: "First they tell me I should close anytime, and now they tell me I have to be sure I don't mistime when I close. Which am I supposed to believe?" To this day, I'm not sure why these two ideas—which seem so contradictory—would appear together in the same seminar, on the same page.

Like trial closing, ABC is not entirely without merit. Not only does it underscore the importance of positive mental preparation, it also helps us become better at knowing when a prospect is ready to commit. However, the problem with ABC is that it can compel salespeople to close much earlier and much more often than they should.

If you attempt to close too early in the leasing process, people will almost always say no. And when people say no, they become very difficult to change. You see, in order for a person to change their no to a yes, they basically have to admit they were wrong in the first place. People aren't generally inclined to make that sort of admission, especially to someone they may perceive as a pushy salesperson. On the other hand, if you

attempt to close too often, people tend to feel pressured and annoyed. Most prospects are very reluctant to lease apartments—or buy anything, for that matter—from people who adopt a hard-sell mentality like the one promoted by ABC.

Assumptive Closing

For years, one of the most widely endorsed closing techniques in the apartment industry has been the "Assumptive Close." Assumptive closing—when the assumption is made that a prospect will lease whether they've said they want to or not—is such a time-honored tradition that its validity is rarely questioned. Make no mistake. In the right hands, assumptive closing can be very, very effective. But like trial closing and ABC, it can also produce dismal results.

Here's why: Assuming someone will lease an apartment is an incredibly risky game to play. If I were to guess, I'd say you don't like people making up your mind for you any more than I like people making up my mind for me. If someone's trying to decide something for me, it's probably because they'll get something, like a commission, if I roll over and go along. That makes it tough for me to trust them, because I know that my money is motivating them more than anything else. In other words, there's a good chance I'm being manipulated.

What's worse is that assumptive closing often results in lease cancellations. Using high-powered assumptive methods, strong leasing professionals can literally sweep prospects off their feet, which isn't necessarily bad. The problem occurs afterward, when those same prospects have the opportunity to reflect on what happened. If they feel that the leasing representative was more responsible for the decision than they were, they're likely to experience buyer's remorse, and as we saw in Secret 3, buyer's remorse can be a major factor behind lease cancellations.

To its credit, assumptive closing does have advantages. Leasing professionals who master its finer points absolutely *radiate* self-confidence, which in turn helps raise the confidence of the prospect. Making an assumptive comment like, "Let's take this one off the market for you now" can be a remarkably effective thing to do, provided the necessary foundation of trust and respect has been established beforehand. As long as care is taken not to pressure or manipulate, assumptive closing can be highly magnetic and hard to resist.

Urgency Closing

The "Urgency Close" is responsible for more customer mistrust and suspicion than any other technique used in apartment leasing today. The main idea behind urgency closing is to create anxiety in the future resident, by emphasizing the downsides of delaying their decision to lease.

The urgency close, in most of its forms, is extremely manipulative. It preys on people's fears, and while some sales experts would maintain that fear is a legitimate means of motivating people to buy, in this author's opinion it is not. If we have to scare people into leasing apartments from us, then frankly we don't deserve their business.

Another major problem with urgency closing is that it tempts salespeople to lie. Examples of the lies that are told in the attempt to create urgency include classics like this: "You know, someone was *just* in here looking at this apartment, but they didn't leave a deposit. If you want it, you'd better move fast." Or how about this: "Oh man, you're lucky you came in today. This is the *last one I have*." It's enough to make you wonder: Is it truth? Or is it fiction?

When we cut through the deception that so often surrounds the urgency close, we find that there is indeed something that can strengthen our closing approach. That something involves giving people legitimate reasons to take action, and it is explained further in the upcoming section, "Offer Reassurance."

Gimmicks

You've probably heard of them before: The Ice Cream Cookie Close, the White Rabbit Close, and the Double-Okay Close, among others. Now yes, some people invent clever methods for asking prospects to lease, and some of them apparently work. On the other hand, it's important to realize that many (if not most) apartment shoppers are *extremely wary* of being subjected to sales gimmickry.

Not long ago, I decided to experiment with an old sales gimmick. A good friend of mine was in the process of making a career decision, and I was trying to help him out. So, I pulled out a piece of paper and began using what's known as the "Ben Franklin" or "Balance Sheet" Close. The idea is to start by drawing a large T on a sheet of paper, which in effect forms two columns. Working together with your prospect (or in this case my friend) you list the disadvantages of deciding a certain way in the left column. Then, you list the advantages on the right. As the theory goes, if you can list more *advantages* on the right side than you can *disadvantages* on the left, you can convince just about anyone of anything.

Well, evidently anyone but Andy. In fact, old Ben Franklin got caught red-handed. In an irritated tone of voice, Andy said, "Oh *come on*—I don't need you to write it down. Don't you think I know what I'm dealing with here? If I wanted to look at my situation on paper, believe me, I'd put it there myself."

I wish I could say I was surprised, but I wasn't.

Please don't misunderstand. If you have a particularly ingenious method for leasing apartments, and it works, by all means keep using it. However, the important point to remember is that there is no reason to feel inadequate if you don't use leasing gimmicks. If gimmicks aren't your style, and for a large percentage of us they are not, then kick back and enjoy. This chapter was written especially for you.

FIVE STEPS TO CLOSING SUCCESS

The first thing to remember in relation to closing (or inviting, which as you've noticed by now is the term I use whenever possible) is that the prospect is not your adversary. Prospects come to you because they *want* to lease an apartment—not because they don't. The only real question is whether they'll lease from you, or whether they'll lease from one of your competitors. Now granted, the competition may have availability when you do not, but in most cases (assuming everything else is equal) the answer to this question boils down to one basic truth: People will lease an average apartment from someone they like before they will lease a breathtaking apartment from someone they don't.

However, becoming a more likable person is only half of what it takes to strengthen your ability to close. The other half requires building a solid foundation of knowledge and skill. For the sake of the following discussion, we're going to assume that optimism and enthusiasm are traits you already possess. Therefore, we're going to concentrate from this point forward on ways you can increase your knowledge, and develop better skills in the art of closing.

Assuming that you have an available apartment of the type your prospect wants, and assuming also that your prospect is qualified in every regard, you can dramatically increase your closing ratios by following these five proven steps:

Recognize Leasing Signals
Reinforce Leasing Signals
Measure Interest
Offer Reassurance
Extend an Invitation

Recognize Leasing Signals

When people are enthused about an apartment, they will more often than not express positive indications of their interest. These are known as *leasing signals*. Some are obvious, and some are more subtle. By listening carefully and watching closely, you'll be able to recognize leasing signals and use them to your advantage

Leasing signals appear in two different forms—verbal and nonverbal.

Verbal leasing signals. Verbal leasing signals are positive indications of genuine interest. When a prospect makes enthusiastic comments, asks specific questions, agrees with what you say, answers questions in the affirmative, or responds to suggestions favorably, chances are extremely good that their level of interest in the apartment is high.

Some verbal leasing signals you're likely to hear include:

"I really like this [feature or benefit.]"
"Can I get this same floorplan with [a different color carpet, a view, etc.]?"
"This would be a huge improvement over where I live now."

"Where would I park?"

"How much do I need to put down?"

"Let's see, I could put my couch right here, and my end tables there . . ." (placing furniture)

"This will be MY bedroom . . . This can be OUR office . . ." (use of possessive pronouns)

Nonverbal leasing signals. The messages people send through their facial expressions and body language are often as powerful, if not more so, than the messages they send in their words. When their level of interest is strong, you'll notice that your prospect:

- Is calm, at ease, and exhibits no signs of wanting to leave
- Demonstrates a comfortable posture—arms uncrossed, hands at rest, frequent smiles, etc.
- Shows a positive attitude toward you and the thought of living in the apartment
- Maintains steady eye contact and/or nods in agreement when you are speaking
- Makes detailed notes or brief calculations
- Physically draws closer as you explain finer details
- Reaches for an application and begins reviewing it

Reinforce Leasing Signals

Once your prospects have demonstrated their interest by way of leasing signals—whether verbal, nonverbal, or both—you want to respond with positive reinforcement. The better people feel about the decision they're preparing to make, the more likely they'll be to say yes.

When someone sends you a leasing signal like, "My dining set would fit really nicely in here." *reinforce what they've said*. Using the first Magic Question, ask them to describe the set for you. Then reinforce their comment by telling them they're right: "You know, I think you're right. Based on how you just described it, your dining set *would* look great in this room."

You can also reinforce leasing signals nonverbally. When your prospect gives a positive indication, nod your head in agreement. Smile. Use positive gestures, like a "thumbs up" or "OK" sign. Or, depending on the personality of the prospect, congratulate your prospect's good ideas with a handshake or a "high five." Communicate through body language of your own that you're excited about helping them make a good decision.

From now on, whenever you recognize verbal or nonverbal leasing signals, enthusiastically reinforce them. Continue asking open-ended questions like, "What else did you have in mind? What other things might you put in this room? How do you feel about [whatever]?" Demonstrate interest in ideas they've brought up. Tune in to their emotions, and mirror their level of excitement. When you recognize and reinforce leasing signals, you create an atmosphere of positive energy that will help *everyone* get what they want.

Measure Interest

Throughout the leasing presentation, it helps to ask questions that periodically measure your prospect's level of interest. There are two reasons for this. First, if the prospect has little or no interest in the apartment you're showing, there's not much point in wasting any more of their time or yours. Second, if you sense that the prospect is interested, but you're not sure how strongly, then you want to make sure that you don't jump the gun (see "ABC").

As the presentation unfolds, measuring questions help you determine the best course of action to take. Here are some effective questions you can ask to measure your prospect's interest:

"Is this starting to look like what you had in mind?"
"Do you think this [bedroom, storage, etc.] would work for you?"
"Does it seem like we're on the right track?"
"How do you feel about everything so far?"

Notice that the first three measuring questions are yes/no questions. They give the prospect complete freedom to say either yes or no, thoroughly unlike the manipulative trial closing questions mentioned in a previous section. The fourth measuring question is designed to help reveal your prospect's level of emotional involvement; as we saw in Secret 3, feelings and emotions play an important role in people's decisions to lease. When next you have the opportunity, ask measuring questions. They will

help you know when to stop—and more important, when and how to proceed.

Offer Reassurance

When prospects approach the point of having to make a decision, tension can build inside them. Like most people faced with committing large sums of money, prospects often experience a rush of anxiety. Though they may never come out and say anything, in their minds they may be silently asking themselves questions like, "Can I really afford this apartment?" "What if I move in and decide I don't like it?" Or, "Will my spouse/roommate approve?"

If we ask people to lease before we've calmed their anxieties, it's possible that we'll drive them away. That's why reassuring our prospects before asking them to lease is such a worthwhile investment of our time and energies. There are a number of ways this can be done.

- *Focus your complete attention on the prospect.* Your prospects want to know that they are important. They want to know that you are focused on them and their situation alone. However, if you allow yourself to be distracted by other matters, your prospects can feel insulted. If they think they're unimportant to you, or low on your list of priorities, they can disappear in the blink of an eye. To prevent this from happening, give prospects your complete and undivided attention. As long as they're at the center of your focus, they'll be more inclined to feel like you've earned the right to their business.
- *Bring out the application in advance.* Prospects have been known to freeze when the application is brought out. Even though it's only an application, in their mind it's "The Contract," and contracts mean commitment. To prevent anxious reactions when you present the application, keep a copy in plain sight throughout the leasing encounter. Whether you're in the office or a vacant apartment, refer to it now and again. Point out some of its most important elements. Make it a nonthreatening part of the process. In short, get your prospect accustomed to the sight of it. Doing so will greatly reduce the chance they'll resist when you invite them to fill it out.

- *Summarize key benefits*. One of the most reassuring things you can do for a prospect in the midst of a big decision is to summarize the things they like best. During your demonstration, your prospect saw things that they liked, and things they did not. However, most people realize that there is no such thing as a perfect apartment, and that small compromises will have to be made no matter where they choose to live. Before inviting your prospects to lease, take a brief moment to summarize the things they liked the most. Keep a running list of their favorite things, like the view, the brick fireplace, the play area, the pool, or whatever. Then review the list out loud, once again creating a mental motion picture that features them in the starring role. Summarizing helps take people's minds off the compromises they have to make, and further reassures them of the reasons your apartment fits best.
- *Give people valid reasons to take action*. In an earlier discussion on urgency, we saw how urgency techniques are often very manipulative. Many people cringe at the thought of being subjected to such manipulation, and you should be acutely aware of that. However, since your job is to lease apartments, you must also secure commitments from as many prospects as you can. So, instead of creating urgency, think of giving your prospects **valid reasons to take action now**. If the reasons you give are legitimate, your prospects will feel reassured that you are trustworthy, and that you have their best interests at heart. Regardless of what your occupancy level may be, here are a pair of excellent reasons you can offer to reassure people and encourage them to action:

"In order for me to have everything ready by your move-in date, I'd need to start pulling it all together right away . . . "

or,

"The only way I can guarantee someone else won't get this apartment is with a deposit. And since it looks like it could be a good fit, a deposit might be the best thing to do . . . "

From this point forward, do your best to eliminate hard-sell urgency techniques from your leasing approach. Instead, give people valid and honest reasons to take action. That way, they'll know they're making the best possible decision—and so will you.

Extend an Invitation

Have you been searching for the great and magical secret to closing success? If so, today's your lucky day, because here it is:

> ***Ask, and you shall receive. If you don't ask, you won't receive.***

Bottom line, that's about as magical as it gets.

This secret is about one thing, and one thing only—ways you can sharpen your ability to close. However, before we get into the specifics of what closing really is, we must first define what closing is *not*.

1. Giving your prospect an application, then instructing them to fill it out and bring it back with their deposit is not closing;
2. Waiting for your prospect to say, "I'll take it!" is not closing;
3. Handing prospects a business card and telling them to call as soon as they decide is not closing;
4. Asking "What do you think?" at the end of a presentation is not closing.

Rather, genuine closing is defined as *asking the prospect for a commitment*. There is no other way around it—ask means ask. But how? Some people get caught up in a fruitless search for a mystical phrase, hoping one day they'll discover words they can memorize and use without fail for the rest of time. Forget it. There is no such thing as a "one size fits all" closing technique. Nor are there any magical formulas, contrary to what numerous writers of sales wizardry would have you believe. Closing is an ever changing, multi-faceted process. It is different for every apartment you demonstrate. And it is different with every prospect you meet.

While there are undoubtedly countless other ways of doing so, this book contains three sensible, practical, and proven ways to ask your prospect to lease.

The Direct Invitation. Far and away, the fastest route to gaining a commitment from your prospect is to come right out and ask for it. In other words, don't beat around the bush. Be courteous, of course, but be direct. If you believe that an apartment fits what your prospect is looking for, and you've spent a sufficient amount of time establishing a relationship of trust, then inviting your prospect to lease should be no more stressful than asking a good friend to dinner.

However, for some the direct approach seems unsophisticated, or even too abrupt. It's no wonder. For years, the sales gurus of America have been telling us that we need to ask this type of question in so-and-so a situation, and that type of question in such-and-such. The "experts" have bent over backward to complicate a process that really need not be complicated at all.

That, admittedly, is a bold statement to make. However, it is well-illustrated by the stories of three different sales professionals who were interviewed during the research phase of this book. Their credentials are impressive. Each is currently generating annual sales in the millions of dollars, and each enjoys a very sizable income. All were asked this question: "What's your best closing technique?" Are you ready for this? To a person, they said they didn't know.

They didn't know! How could this be? It certainly couldn't have been because they never close. No, closing is something these people do with extraordinary skill and consistency. Once they began describing their methods of operation, however, the picture became quite clear. To summarize, each of these salespeople begins the selling process by asking their prospects a series of customer-focused questions, listening carefully to each response. In this fashion, they become knowledgeable about their prospects' priorities, needs, and unique characteristics. Next, they present information about their product—but only information that is particularly relevant to needs or preferences the prospect has expressed. And finally, once all questions are answered and all objections are resolved, *they simply ask for the business*. No fanfare. No miracle phrases or amazing one-liners. No beating around the bush. They just cut to the chase and ask.

And you can do the same, with questions like these:

"Is this what you had in mind?"
"Do you feel like this apartment would work?"
"Shall we take this one off the market?"
"With a security deposit of $_____, we can put your name on this one now. How does that sound?"
"All things considered, this apartment seems to be an excellent fit. What do you say?"
And so on, and so on, and so on. . . .

If people truly want to lease, nothing will reveal the fact more quickly than giving them the opportunity to say yes. Forget about using sophisticated, sugar-coated phrases. They do little more than make people nervous and trip them up. Besides, you *know* this person. If you've built a solid relationship, you've earned the right to be direct. So make it easy on yourself, and on your prospect. Use the direct invitation approach. You'll lease more apartments in less time than ever before.

The Temporary Hold. Provided there are no laws or company restrictions to prevent you from doing otherwise, the temporary hold is a remarkably effective way to invite your prospects to lease. Here's how it works: Let's say a prospect is interested in the apartment, but for some reason they resist with a deflection or two. Maybe they want to "think it over." Or maybe they have "a couple more places to look at." Your response using the temporary hold approach might sound something like this:

> *"I can appreciate that you want to think things over. And really you should—you're making a big decision. However, I'd hate to see you miss an opportunity to lease this apartment, because I think we both agree that it fits what you're looking for.*
>
> *"Tell you what . . . since we need some sort of deposit to prevent another person from leasing this apartment, why don't you put down a temporary hold deposit. For just [let's say $100], we can take this apartment off the market until [whatever time] tomorrow. That way, at least you'll know you have*

a place that works. You can breathe a little easier and have the additional time you need. Does that sound like a fair deal?"

The beauty of offering a temporary hold is that it creates a level of commitment while giving the prospect whatever room they need to think. In addition, the prospect basically gets the best of both worlds. So, if you recommend a temporary hold and your prospect agrees, congratulate them on their wise decision. Write a receipt for the amount they put down (usually no less than $50), thank them graciously, and encourage them to go home and relax. Tell them you're glad they found something they like. And invite them to call if they have further questions. Handle everything as efficiently and enthusiastically as you can. More than anything, *make them feel really, really good about the decision they made.*

One last note on using the temporary hold. Reserving apartments with the full security deposit is always preferable to accepting a temporary hold. The more money a person puts down, the stronger their commitment will typically be. So start by asking for the full deposit. If your prospect balks at the idea, then guess what? You've got the temporary hold as your "ace in the hole."

The Alternate Choice. The alternate choice approach is very effective when you've got more than one apartment to lease. The idea behind the alternate choice is to demonstrate a limited number of suitable apartments, say two or three, and then invite the prospect to lease the one he or she likes best.

As we've seen, resentment can develop when salespeople try to make up their prospects' minds without their permission. Prospects want to know that *they*, and not the salesperson, have determined how their money will be spent. If, for example, you've shown your prospect two different apartments, begin by asking what they liked best about each. Then give them the alternate choice: *"We've got a couple of great options for you to choose from. Which one do you think would work best?"*

An alternate choice question like this will result in either one of two possible outcomes. One, your prospect will immediately choose one apartment over the other, in which case the alternate choice method was an instant success. Or, your prospect will balk, in which case you'll need to

ask more questions. If this happens, don't be disappointed; more dialogue will help you further clarify what the prospect wants, and keep the door open for another try.

There are two major advantages in giving people the freedom to choose. Number one, the prospect does almost all of the work; they convince themselves and arrive at *wanting* the apartment with minimal input from us. Number two, prospects who select one apartment over another are far less likely to cancel once their decision has been made. The reason is because *they* controlled the decision (even though you more or less controlled the process leading up to it). When you respect people enough to let them make up their own minds, they like you more. And as we've seen time and again, people prefer doing business with people they like.

So go ahead—be willing to afford people the freedom to choose. As long as they get what they want, you'll get what you want.

AFTER THE INVITATION . . .

Tell your prospects they are wanted. A successful businesswoman recently told me of the experience she had in leasing her new apartment. She had shopped a number of apartment communities, and had seen three different apartments that suited her tastes just fine. However, as is so often the case, she ultimately decided to lease *where she felt most wanted.* The apartment she selected was presented by a dynamic leasing representative, who invited Ann to lease by saying this: "Ann, I know you like this apartment. And I know you would really enjoy living here. What do you say we set this one aside? *We'd love to have you as a neighbor.*" Not surprisingly, Ann wholeheartedly accepted the invitation. Who wouldn't?

There's a twofold lesson we can learn from this story. First, it illustrates the point that people lease apartments from people they like. Second, it reminds us that everybody, in some measure or another, wants to *feel wanted.* Make an effort to tell qualified prospects that you want them to lease. Just be sure that when you say it, you mean it.

Be quiet. A friend recently invited me to escort her to a wedding. She began with a straightforward explanation of her circumstances, reviewing all the details including date, time, and location. She then politely asked if I would be willing to go with her. "Sounds pretty good," I thought to myself. Just as I was about to accept her invitation, she surprised me by saying, "It's okay if you don't want to go. If it doesn't work for you, I'll totally understand."

Hmmmm. All of a sudden, things began to sound less appealing. Why *wouldn't* I want to go? Why *wouldn't* it work for me? I started asking questions. The more questions I asked, the more flustered she got. And to be honest, I started looking for a way to say no. It wasn't because I didn't want to be her escort. It wasn't that at all. It was because what initially sounded like something I wanted to do had now been darkened by a shadow of doubt. If she had only been quiet long enough to let me say yes, the sudden rush of uncertainty I experienced could have been completely avoided.

When you ask our prospect a crucial closing question, you must be patient and wait for their reply. You've heard the old adage: The first person who speaks loses. Well, it's true. Besides, people can't say yes if you're talking. Once you've asked your closing question, *don't say another word until you get a response*. Even if it takes five minutes, and even if you feel like you'll die in the silence, wait. Not only is waiting the considerate thing to do, in that it gives your prospect the opportunity to reply, but it's wise. It keeps you from putting your foot in your mouth and undoing what you've worked so hard to accomplish.

Offer a little privacy. Many times people want to discuss the implications of their decision in private; a moment alone when weighing big decisions can be greatly appreciated. Even if your prospects don't ask for time to themselves, it may be appropriate to offer it anyway.

> *"Why don't I leave you alone, so you can talk things over in private? I'll come back in a few minutes. If you need anything in the meantime, I'll be right around the corner. Just let me know."*

When you give people space, you indirectly tell them that you have no intention of pressuring them into a decision. In fact, the power of reverse psychology comes into play when you offer a moment of privacy to your prospects. Whereas at first they may have expected you to try talking them

into something, they now have no reason to be defensive. By giving them space you've basically said, "Even though I know this is the right apartment for you, I'm going to let you reach that conclusion on your own. I want you to lease this apartment, which is why I'm not going to pressure you about it." If you believe it might make the difference, offer people a little time to themselves. It's a rare indication of respect and confidence that won't go unnoticed.

WHAT TO DO WHEN YOUR PROSPECT SAYS "YES"

Ask "Are you sure?" Some salespeople, upon hearing their prospect say yes, start walking on eggshells, hoping that they won't change their mind. This is an absolutely, positively undignified thing to do. Reckless as it may sound, what often works best is to make your prospect tell you they want the apartment, just so they can hear themselves say it.

The next time someone leases an apartment from you, ask them, "*Are you sure?*" If they have *truly* committed to leasing that apartment, asking them if they're sure about it will not change things a bit. If anything, it will deepen their desire even more, because in a subtle way you're challenging them to defend their judgment. But let's say, for the sake of argument, that you ask your prospect, "Are you sure?" and they say no. Is all hope lost? Of course not. If the prospect says no, then the question has simply shed light on the fact that they still have some concerns. When do you want to find this out? Here and now, when you can get whatever it is resolved and out of the way? Or later, after buyer's remorse has settled in and the prospect wants to cancel?

Do not be afraid to ask this question. Yes, it may take you outside your comfort zone at first, and yes, it may come as a surprise to your prospect. That's to be expected. But if zero cancellations and confident, loyal residents are your goal, hold your head high and ask, "*Are you sure?*"

Remain composed. When a prospect says yes, you may experience a powerful temptation to overflow with thanksgiving and relief. Although this is completely natural, you must exercise self-control. Keep your emotions in check. People are very aware of salespeople's reactions when a deal is made, and a look of surprise or elation can bring doubt to a prospect's mind. They may start asking themselves, "Does she look surprised because I *actually* leased *this* apartment? Is leasing this apartment such a good idea after all?"

These, of course, are questions you do not want your prospects to contemplate. So in the excitement of your big success, do your best to remain poised and steady. And by all means, maintain a manner of professional courtesy. Remember to offer refreshments, and make them feel at home. Save the celebration until after they have completed their application, given you their deposit, and left. Then, if you feel like dancing on the desk, go for it.

Make yourself available. Rarely does a person lease an apartment and not have questions afterward. However, after they've placed their deposit and gone home, people are sometimes reluctant to call. Out of courtesy, they may not want to disturb you. Or they may think their question would sound dumb. You can strengthen the bridge between you and your prospects by inviting them to call and making yourself available, no matter what. Remember: Not only have you just made an important commitment to serve this customer, but you've also been rewarded with business that could easily have been granted to Brand X down the street. For that reason, build the confidence of your new residents by demonstrating your willingness to serve. Let them know you'll be there, if and when they need you.

Show your appreciation. There is absolutely no way that you can show people too much gratitude. Giving heartfelt, sincere appreciation is one of the best ways you'll ever find to win the good favor of others. So, a few days after your prospect agrees to lease, send them a tangible expression of your appreciation. Mail a personalized "CONGRATULATIONS!" card signed by all your staff. Have a carnation or bouquet of balloons delivered to their place of work. Send them a small housewarming gift, like a plant or a gift basket. Be professional, of course, but don't be shy. Use your imagination! And never make the mistake of thinking you have to spend a lot of money. As our mothers always said, it's the *thought* that counts.

WHAT TO DO WHEN YOUR PROSPECT SAYS "NO"

Try, try again! Thomas Edison, the famous inventor of the electric light bulb, once said: "Many of life's failures are people who did not realize how close they were to success when they gave up." How very true. In apartment leasing, as with many other things in life, there are times when leasing professionals give up too easily.

While we never want to pester people whose minds are made up, we don't want to just roll over and accept defeat, either. So if your prospect declines your first invitation, don't give up. Try, try again! It's not as hard as you might think. All you need is a little faith in yourself, and the courage to ask a simple question, depending on the nature of your prospect. The next time you have a prospect who declines your invitation, here are some ideas to help you stay in the game.

"Is there something I've overlooked?"
"What is it about the apartments we've seen that you don't like?"
"Is there something I haven't explained to your satisfaction?"
"Could you describe for me what it is you're really looking for?"
"What would it take for this apartment to work?"
And so on, and so on, and so on. . . .

As long as your prospect is not completely rigid in their refusal, try to keep the dialogue moving. Granted, you may find that despite your best and most enthusiastic efforts, the apartment just won't work. But you could *just as easily* find out that your prospect isn't so against the idea after all. Your question may uncover a hidden objection that you possess the ability to resolve. Or, it may reveal a concern that you can gently bring to rest.

The point is that you'll never know how close you are unless you try again. No matter what the outcome may be, trying again will let you know inside your heart that you gave it the very best shot you could.

In the end, if people absolutely refuse to lease, know this: As long as you don't get pushy, you have *every right* to ask your prospects why they've said no. Maybe they'll tell you. Maybe they won't. It doesn't matter—ask, and try to learn from the experience. Finding the courage

will help you grow stronger. And finding the answers will help you grow *smarter*.

WHAT TO DO WHEN YOUR PROSPECT SAYS "I'LL BE BACK"

Sometimes a prospect will demonstrate an encouraging level of interest, only to say that they need to come back. While at the moment it may be frustrating, and while we must be sure that every qualified prospect we meet receives an invitation, some people simply will not commit until first they're given the freedom to leave. As Dale Carnegie pointed out in the quote that begins this chapter, we can't make people do what they don't want to do. They have to want to do the thing themselves, and if wanting an apartment means they need to leave and come back again, who are we to argue?

I recently had the pleasure of working with the staff at an apartment community in Phoenix. In the first fifteen days of one particular month they leased seven apartments, *four* of which were to "be backs"—people who refused to put down a deposit on their initial visit. The moral to the story is that while it *is* a sin to let someone drive away without doing everything possible to earn their business on their first visit, it is *not* a sin to let a person leave if they feel they must come back. Some people absolutely will not place a deposit on the first visit, no matter how much they like what they see. Besides, pressuring them otherwise would be a huge mistake.

You can increase your odds of leasing to "be backs" by doing four things. First, demonstrate sincere interest in helping them find what's best for them, no matter how long it takes. Second, present the cleanest and most appealing apartments you can; leave no doubt in their mind that you'll be ready when they are. Third, when they drive away, make sure they have your business card and a brochure on which you've written and highlighted the things you want them to remember most. And, fourth, stay in touch by following up (see Secret 7). The more you demonstrate your willingness to serve, and the more you respect their timetable, the more likely you are to win the business of "be backs."

WHAT TO DO WHEN *YOU* MUST SAY NO

Most apartment communities process lease applications with a credit reporting service. These services research and, in most cases, verify an applicant's employment, their income, their rental history, and their credit rating.

Let's say that you've just taken an application from a prospect. You submit it to your screening company, and they return the verdict: *Deny occupancy*. When this happens, it's very important your prospect be properly informed. Not only must you remain impartial, but you must also allow denied prospects to maintain their dignity.

Here's an evenhanded way to break the bad news. When notifying an applicant that their application has been turned down, never tell the person that *they* have been denied. Instead, tell the person that their *application* has been denied, based on information contained in the credit report. In addition, never allow yourself to be drawn into a discussion concerning the reasons for denial. Instead, politely provide your applicant with the name and number of the company that generated the report, and leave it at that.

You want to avoid debates with unqualified applicants at all costs. However, the reason may not be as obvious as you think. The unqualified applicant of today could very well become the qualified applicant of next month or next year. While you shouldn't ignore the warning signs of a high-risk applicant, don't be hasty in your decisions to deny. People bounce back, and in the long run, it pays to be courteous and kind.

THE GREATEST LEASING SECRET OF ALL

One of the biggest myths about successful apartment leasing is that in order to become a champion, you need to be able to talk people into leasing apartments. Well, I've got good news. Nothing could be further from the truth.

In fact, you're better off not trying to talk people into anything. Whenever you try talking someone into leasing an apartment, there's an almost unavoidable tendency to apply pressure. And when people feel pressured, they usually don't lease.

Therefore, if the thought of closing has made you nervous in the past, take heart. Success in apartment leasing isn't about pressure. It's about giving people an invitation to do what you've helped them determine they want to do. When you begin looking at things from this point of view, you'll be well on your way to discovering the greatest leasing secret of all:

The secret to success in apartment leasing doesn't lie in your ability to persuade. It lies in your ability to serve.

REVIEW

Perhaps the most important factor in the apartment leasing equation is inviting your prospects to lease. It is your responsibility to see that *every qualified prospect you meet* receives an invitation to lease. You can lease more apartments than ever before by keeping these important considerations in mind:

- Recognize the various strengths and weaknesses of the apartment industry's traditional closing techniques:

  Trial Closing
  ABC (Always Be Closing)
  Assumptive Closing
  Urgency Closing
  Gimmicks

- Study and apply the principles in each of the five steps to closing success:

  Recognize verbal and nonverbal leasing signals
  Positively reinforce leasing signals when they appear
  Periodically measure the extent of your prospect's interest
  Offer reassurance that your prospect is making a good decision
  Give your prospect the opportunity to say yes—invite them to lease

- After you've extended the invitation:

  Tell your prospects that they are wanted
  Be quiet
  Offer a little privacy

- When your prospect says "yes":

  Ask, "*Are you sure?*"
  Remain composed
  Make yourself available
  Show your appreciation

- When your prospect says "no," by all means, try again!
- When your prospect says, "I'll be back," remember that you cannot make a person do something they are not yet willing to do themselves. Commit to helping them as they continue their search, and by all means, stay in touch.
- When *you* must say no, instead of informing people that *they've* been denied tell them that their *application* has been denied. Never discuss the contents of a credit report with a denied applicant. If they request information, refer them to the service that generated their report.
- Remember that the greatest leasing secret of all is that you don't have to worry about talking people into anything. The secret to success in leasing doesn't lie in your ability to persuade. It lies in your ability to serve.

Secret Number 7

Follow-Up Is the Extra Mile of Apartment Leasing

Things may come to those who wait, but only the things left by those who hustle.

Abraham Lincoln

For just a moment, think back to the previous secret and the Phoenix apartment community mentioned there. At that property, almost 60 percent of the apartments leased in a two-week period were leased to prospects who refused to commit on their first visit. This is a very significant statistic. First, it supports the position that hard-sell leasing techniques are rarely the best prescription for filling vacancies. Second, it demonstrates that some prospects simply will not lease until the leasing professional steps up and "goes the extra mile" to earn their business. As the title of this secret points out, that extra mile is known as *follow-up*.

When shopping for an apartment, a prospect's decision-making cycle can be long and drawn out. It is not uncommon for weeks (or even months) to go by before a prospect reaches their decision. *For Rent Magazine* recently conducted a study which indicated that, on the average,

23 percent of apartment shoppers plan their moves two to four weeks in advance. However, this detail was eclipsed by the finding that nearly 74 percent of apartment shoppers plan their moves six *to* eight *weeks* in advance.

Why do all these people begin looking so far ahead of their move date? Simply put, apartment shoppers are notorious for shopping around. During the typical six-to-eight week process, prospects plan and measure. They bring their roommates, spouses, or children back to look. They calculate drive times, investigate neighborhood services, visit schools, and so forth. And unwilling as we may be to admit it, they visit the competition as well. There are a huge number of variables that figure into moving, and all of them are not always settled in the prospect's mind after just one visit to just one community.

So what happens? In many cases, people look and then they leave. It happens all the time, often in spite of our best efforts to have them do otherwise. And this is where follow-up comes into the picture. If a prospect is qualified, and their level of interest is reasonably strong at the time they leave, you still stand a good chance of leasing to them after all. Follow-up—*that process by which you continue contacting prospects who have not yet leased in an ongoing attempt to earn their business*—is the best way to increase your odds of achieving future success.

TURNING THE TABLES

It is interesting to note that follow-up feels somewhat unnatural to many in our profession. In large part, the reason is because follow-up turns the tables. Instead of the prospect calling the leasing professional (which is the direction that leasing communication almost always travels) follow-up requires that the leasing professional call the prospect. Yes, there are occasions when we leave our offices to promote our properties in the marketplace, but rarely if ever do we complete lease transactions this way. The actual business we generate, in the vast majority of cases, is made possible only because *the prospective resident has chosen to contact us*. Therefore, since follow-up goes against the typical flow of communication, it has a tendency to make leasing professionals feel uncomfortable. Put another way, it feels like cold calling, which few in the selling professions can honestly say they enjoy.

Whether follow-up makes us uncomfortable or not, the reality in apartment leasing today is that consistent follow-up can spell the difference between success and disaster. Not long ago, a property manager told of a distressed apartment community she'd been asked to help turn around. With 350 apartments, the property's vacancy rate was 20 percent—and climbing. After carefully analyzing its current leasing procedures, she discovered that one of the property's biggest problems was that no follow-up had been conducted by the leasing staff for over *three months*. Even worse, overall vacancy rates for the surrounding market area were holding steady at 4 percent. The competition was having a field day at their expense, due in large part to the fact that a consistent follow-up program had not been maintained.

Survival of the Fittest

Consistently soliciting prospects with strong future potential is quite possibly the most reliable way to compete—and remain competitive—in the apartment leasing arena. Recently, the sales manager of a Fortune 500 company used the following analogy to vividly emphasize the critical importance of holding a competitive edge:

"Every morning on the plains of Africa, a gazelle wakes up. The gazelle knows that it must run faster than the fastest lion, or it will be killed by sundown. Every morning on the same plain, a lion wakes up. The lion knows that it must run faster than the slowest gazelle, or it will starve to death. So, it doesn't matter if you're a lion or a gazelle. When the sun comes up, you'd better hit the ground running."

In order to keep from being devoured in today's competitive market, you must never let up in your leasing efforts. In other words, you must hit the ground running every single day, sending correspondence, making callbacks, and doing whatever else you can to eventually win the business of qualified prospects who come and go. Remember, your competitors are vying for the very same prospects as you. But you can outperform the competition, *if you consistently do the things they're not likely to do themselves*. Follow-up falls into that category. It is the apartment leasing superstar's little known secret of success.

WHY FOLLOW UP?

Again, the whole point of follow-up is to eventually earn the business of qualified prospects who insist on having more time to decide. It is a short-term investment in effort that carries the potential for long-term payoffs down the road. In a number of exciting ways, consistent follow-up gives a tremendous leasing advantage to those who appreciate the results it can produce.

Follow-up helps generate higher returns on advertising investments. Never let anyone tell you that advertising is an expense. It is not. Advertising, of any kind, is an *investment*. When dollars are spent to pay expenses, it usually involves a straight-forward exchange of cash for products or services of equal value. For example, if you need office supplies, you pay what they cost, the expense is recorded, and the supplies become yours. Nothing more, nothing less.

Advertising dollars, on the other hand, are uniquely different. They have the potential to produce *returns* that exceed their beginning value. Provided the advertising we buy is properly targeted, sufficiently well-designed, and delivered adequately to the marketplace, the dollars we invest are likely to come back to us multiplied in the form of additional revenue.

Let's say that your property invests $600 in an ad, and one qualified prospect responds. You win that prospect's business, and they sign a 12-month lease. If the monthly amount on the apartment you leased is $700, your initial $600 advertising investment will ultimately produce $8,400 ($700 × 12 months) in annual rent revenue to your community. An $8,400 return on a $600 initial investment equals an astonishing 1,400 percent return. Try finding that kind of performance on Wall Street.

When you consistently follow-up, especially with prospects who first responded to your advertising in the marketplace, you improve the odds that your advertising investments will bring you the returns you expect. Not only that, it also means you'll know where best to invest your valuable advertising dollars in the future.

Follow-up counteracts prospect procrastination. Of all the forces working against you when prospects leave without committing, procrastination may be the toughest. No matter how interested a prospect may be, the energy and urgency which had been moving them toward a decision quickly fades once they drive away. Unfortunately for them, what procrastinating prospects often don't realize is that this can result in a dangerously false sense of security. Making the decision on where to live and when to move almost always requires more time than people expect.

As leasing professionals, one of our utmost goals should be helping to make positive differences in our prospects' lives. Many times follow-up is the very thing which makes that difference; it may be the only thing helping people avoid a last-minute scramble caused by procrastination. In a way, through follow-up we establish ourselves as a sort of "moving planner," a person who helps lead people in making timely and well-informed decisions. Truthfully, some people (indecisive people, especially) need *and appreciate* a skilled professional who has the ability to help them decide. Follow-up is often the gentle nudge people need to take action and avoid the misery of a poorly planned move.

Your best tool for successfully beating procrastination is *enthusiasm*. During a slow courtship with a prospect, it can be difficult to keep the fires of excitement burning. However, it is in everyone's best interests, especially your prospect's, that you remain enthusiastic about the idea of having them as a new resident. Follow-up fueled by enthusiasm is extraordinarily effective, because *it is virtually impossible to resist an enthusiastic leasing person who genuinely wants to help*. Ask any "shopper" who's tried to walk away from a superstar leaser, and they'll tell you the same thing. If you approach your follow-up efforts with genuine optimism and enthusiasm, your prospects will often respond just the same. In the end, positive energy and proactive follow-up efforts are the keys to neutralizing prospect procrastination.

Follow-up increases awareness of your apartments—and you. When apartment shoppers are moving in high gear, they may have seen so many apartments by the time they reach you that their mind is a blur. As a result, it is quite possible that they will experience information overload and momentarily lose track of who's who—until you make a follow-up contact. When something distinctive arrives from you in their mailbox, or they hear your helpful and interested voice on the phone, you gain an *instant* advantage over your competition.

However, the relationship between your prospect's level of awareness and the amount of time that passes between their visit and your follow-up contact is very important. The more immediate the contact after their visit, the stronger their level of awareness will remain. The longer it takes for follow-up to occur, the weaker their awareness of you and your community will become. That's why *immediacy* is such an important factor in follow-up. It is what keeps the awareness of your community—as well as the need to make a decision—foremost in your prospect's mind.

Follow-up helps reveal hidden objections. As hard as you may have tried to get everything out on the table in the initial visit, it is not uncommon for prospects to leave your office with hidden or unresolved objections. Unfortunately, they are not likely to call the next day and tell you what is wrong. You're going to have to roll up your sleeves and find out for yourself by following up.

In many cases, follow-up is the last chance you have to expose unexpressed objections and remove them as obstacles to future success. This sheds light on yet another reason follow-up takes leasing professionals outside their comfort zone: It increases their odds of having to deal with difficult issues. It also increases their odds of being rejected.

Nevertheless, if objections still remain, you must find them out. The best way to do this is by asking questions. Since it is recommended that follow-up calls begin on a positive note, a question like, "What did you like most about the apartment we saw on Tuesday?" will get things moving in the right direction. Then, if you sense that there is something your prospect isn't disclosing, try to find it out. However, beware of asking prospects to tell you what they don't like. Soliciting negative feedback under any circumstance is risky. Instead, give them an opportunity to speak candidly. Try asking a question like this: *"What else did you have on your mind?"*

This is an exceptionally effective method for revealing hidden objections, because the question is usually answered in one of two ways. The prospect will either say, "Nothing," in which case everything should be okay. Or, the prospect will reveal whatever is on their minds and you'll instantly know what you're up against. Regardless of the response you get, asking this question will help you gain additional ground toward identifying and resolving hidden objections. It will also bring you one step closer to getting that person out for another look.

Follow-up gives you a tremendous competitive edge. Many people in the apartment industry talk about the importance of follow-up. Fortunately for us, not nearly as many put their money where their mouths are. I recently shopped a pair of A-grade apartment communities, both of which were staffed by the leading property management companies in their areas. I chose them fully expecting to find top-caliber leasing performance, including prompt and courteous follow-up. Given who I was dealing with, it seemed a perfectly reasonable thing to expect.

I asked to see one bedrooms at each community, explaining that I was visiting from out of town and was doing some work in the area (true on both counts). Both of the leasing consultants that waited on me were informative, courteous, and genuinely interested in my business—*until* I mentioned that it would be a couple of months before I made my decision.

In both cases it was as if the air conditioning had been switched on. When I qualified myself as a "future" prospect, things suddenly cooled off. The romance disappeared from their eyes. I no longer felt wanted. In a subtle but purely unmistakable way, I started to gather the impression that I wasn't worth their effort.

Okay, I thought. They deserve the benefit of the doubt. Maybe they're just having an off day; it happens to everyone on occasion (although it did seem strange that two different employees of two different management companies on two different properties would be having the same "off day" within an hour of each other). As I finished with each, I made absolutely certain that they had my name, home address, and telephone number. I wanted to be sure they had all the information necessary to conduct what I fully expected would be their usual follow-up.

In the end, though, I wish I could say I was surprised, but I wasn't. From two of the most prestigious apartment communities in the area, I never received a thing. No card. No call. *Nothing*. Now for the sake of discussion, let's say I *was* a real prospect that day, and after visiting those two properties, I'd visited a third: yours. You showed me an apartment, and even though I really liked it, I left without leasing. Soon thereafter, you fol-

lowed up, expressing both your gratitude and a promise to help me find the right apartment no matter what.

Here's the question: Of the three, *who do you think would have earned my business?*

THE THREE ESSENTIAL RULES OF FOLLOW-UP

Before we discuss the "how-tos" of following up with high-probability prospects, we first must cover three essential rules that underlie the success of any follow-up campaign:

First, ***obtain guest cards from every qualified prospect who sees an apartment.*** This means full name, address, and phone numbers for home or place of work. Yes, some prospects are reluctant to give this information, but like extending the invitation, you won't get it if you don't ask for it. There is absolutely no way to establish and maintain an effective follow-up system without completed guest cards. They are the crucial foundation of information upon which we build the success of our efforts.

Second, ***communicate exclusively in terms relevant to your prospect.*** No matter what type of follow-up method you use, make sure it highlights the things that are most important to your prospect. As we have seen, anything you say that doesn't include your prospect is likely to bore them. Make sure your follow-up directly connects the value of the various benefits you offer to their individual wants and needs. Select your words carefully, and clearly state that the value of the quality and service you provide is the best they'll find for their leasing dollar.

Third, ***ask for another commitment.*** As we have seen, the whole purpose of a follow-up campaign is to get people to *take action* and come back out for another look. Remember, when you are dealing with a prospect who is both qualified and interested, the fact that they leave does not mean they're saying no. Rather, it is more likely that they are simply saying "not now." Whether following up with "be back" prospects by mail or by phone, you *must* encourage them to commit to another visit. If you do not, they won't be nearly as inclined to return on their own.

POPULAR METHODS OF FOLLOW-UP

The two most popular, and most effective, methods of follow-up in the apartment industry are *written correspondence* and *telephone calls*. As stated earlier, completed guest cards are absolutely vital to creating and maintaining a consistent follow-up program; frankly, without the details that guest cards provide, effective follow-up is pretty much impossible. In addition to guest cards, many communities also use daily activity logs to record telephone contacts. While they are also an important part of measuring prospect activity, telephone logs are not generally recommended as a means of gathering information for follow-up purposes. The reason is that they rarely provide enough space to record the volume of information needed. Therefore, guest cards are generally preferred for follow-up, because they have more space and address more specific types of detail. And, as we'll see in a moment, they are much better for creating an efficient follow-up system.

In the following sections, we'll begin by examining how to follow up in writing. Next, we'll look at how to follow up by phone. We'll then discuss a way to *combine* written and telephone follow-up methods for maximum effect. Finally, the secrets of a six-step system for consistent follow-up will be revealed as a way to further increase your chances of success.

WRITTEN CORRESPONDENCE

Thank you cards, postcards, and letters are by far the most popular ways to follow up in writing. However, before discussing the ins and outs of each, we first need to put ourselves in our prospects' shoes and think about what generally happens when people go through their mail each day.

When most of us sort our mail, we tend to put it into one of three piles. Let's call these piles A, B, and C. The A pile gets our immediate attention. Anything that even *remotely* resembles a check goes into the A pile, as does correspondence from relatives, spouses, sweethearts, and friends. The B pile is the one we use for items like bills, magazines, and other stuff we decide can wait until later. The last pile, C, is where we put the junk.

Sometimes we don't even bother with making a C pile. We just pull up the garbage can and fire away.

Three Easy Ways to Make the "A Pile"

The objective with written correspondence—whether it's a thank you card, a postcard, or a letter—is to have it wind up in your prospect's A pile. Here's how to do it.

Start with their address. In most cases, you record your prospect's name in the leasing interview. However, with some prospects, requesting an address or phone number at the interview stage can be seen as a bit premature. If you don't get an address, and your prospect has demonstrated interest but is starting to leave, one way or another you're going to have to ask for their address. Not only are you going to have to ask for it, but you're also going to have to gain their permission to use it. If you don't, the correspondence you send may come as an unwelcome surprise, and if that happens it will more than likely wind up in the B pile (or worse.)

If you still haven't gotten your prospect's address, and they're starting to leave, give them a *valid reason* for requesting it—one that demonstrates what's in it for them.

> *"Before you go, let me get your mailing address. I'd just like to stay in touch and continue trying to help however I can. . . ."*

At this point, your chances for getting the address are 50-50, better than if you hadn't asked at all. You *must* try. Too much has been invested not to. (By the way, the same general approach can also be used when requesting telephone numbers.)

However, some people are particularly sensitive and cautious about giving out their addresses. Concern for personal safety is one reason. Fear of being harassed by hardheaded salespeople is another. Giving people legitimate, benefit-oriented reasons for obtaining their address or phone number is the best way to alleviate their anxieties. It demonstrates that your motives are purely honest and professional. Furthermore, it gives your prospect the option of providing a business address if they're wary about giving the one for their home. And if by chance someone gives you a phony address, which does happen, don't worry about it. Let it go and move on to the next opportunity.

Make sure the address is correct and legible. If our mail is to be delivered to the right person on time, it needs to be properly addressed. To ensure the highest likelihood that your prospect will receive the mail you send, double check all addresses for accuracy. Also, make sure that both the mailing and return addresses are legible. The most reliable approach is to carefully print or type everything appearing on the outside of the envelope.

Whatever you send, make it look personal. The more personal-looking you can make your mail, the more likely it is to get opened and read by your prospect. A pile mail exhibits the following characteristics:

- High-quality materials (premium cards or paper stock, matching envelopes, foil applications, etc.)
- Handwritten mailing and return addresses
- First-class postage stamps

From now on, do everything you can to see that whatever you send out winds up in your prospect's A pile. The extra effort doesn't only increase the odds that your mail will be opened. More important, it increases the odds that what you've sent will be *read*.

Writing Thank You Cards

Some management companies print their own thank you cards for the purposes of follow-up. While some are quite well done, others simply are not. It is important to recognize that the correspondence you send from your leasing office is a direct reflection of who you are—not to mention the organization you represent. If the materials you send look first-class, so will you. If they look cheap and mediocre, well . . . the conclusion is yours to draw.

The best policy with thank you cards is to purchase professional quality, high-grade cards from a stationery store. These are the ones featuring gold foil accents, embossed lettering, rich color patterns, custom-matched envelopes, and so forth. When a card like *this* shows up in a prospect's mailbox, it usually doesn't even make it to the front door before it gets opened.

If hundreds or thousands of dollars have been invested in advertising to bring prospects to your door, what sense does it make to pinch pennies in the final stages when you need to impress those people the most? Use only the best quality cards you can find. Much like good advertising, in the long run you'll see returns far in excess of the investments you make.

Finally, thank you cards should be used primarily to *thank*, and not to *sell*. More than anything, your initial follow-up contacts should simply communicate your commitment to helping your prospects get what they want. Since "making a pitch" in the thank you card could potentially interfere with that message, do nothing in the card but express your gratitude. Concentrate first on making whoever receives your card feel warm, recognized, and appreciated. Then, we might add a few words to help "set the stage" for our telephone follow-up efforts (see page 159).

Writing Postcards

If you use postcards for follow-up purposes, use the correct amount of postage. Postcard postage is 20 cents; regular first-class postage is 32 cents. The 12-cent difference may not seem like much up front, but if you send hundreds of postcards a year using first-class postage, the excess can add up fast. That's money that could be used in other promotional efforts, and when it comes to promotion, we need all the firepower we can get.

Keep your message brief. We've all received postcards where the script starts out large and legible, then becomes smaller and more crowded, until finally the reader needs a magnifying glass to finish reading the lines at the bottom. With personal correspondence it's one thing, but with business correspondence it is entirely another. Avoid overcrowding your postcards by drafting what you're going to write on a separate sheet of paper before committing it to the card. Not only can you tailor your message to make every word count, your recipient will find it easier to read.

Writing Letters

Letters work well when you have a substantial amount of information to communicate with your prospect. For example, letters are well-suited to addressing questions concerning your school district, or to explaining community policies or procedures in greater detail. You can also use letters to recap the highlights of your initial conversation, and to re-emphasize key benefits that are particularly well-matched to your prospect.

When writing letters, use company or property letterhead whenever possible. It makes the best and most professional impression, especially since many prospects lease due in part to their perception of the community and/or company you represent.

Another way to strengthen the impact of your letters is to create an appealing list of benefits featured in the apartment your prospect saw. Write a brief description of the things your prospect found most interesting and important during their visit, and include it with your letter. Here's an example:

> Apartment C305 at Colonial Glen is a sunlit, top-floor apartment featuring two bedrooms, two baths, and the following additional conveniences:
>
> - Intercom access for increased privacy
> - Front door with double locks and solid core
> - Neutral gray carpet to suit a range of furnishings and decor
> - Full-size washer/dryer hookups for added convenience
> - 24-hour guaranteed maintenance service
> - Peaceful view of the river trail
> - Nearby covered parking included

It's important to keep in mind that, if your prospect is like most apartment shoppers, they've probably seen a number of other apartments besides yours. Providing them with a benefit sheet summarizing the most desirable aspects of the apartment they liked best will return you and what you offer to the front of their mind. And if you can send something with a photograph to help reinforce those positive images in their mind, so much the better.

Finally, end your letters with a postscript (P.S.). Studies have shown that when a P.S. appears in a letter, it receives higher readership than any other element on the page. The reason is that readers usually expect the

P.S. to contain choice morsels of information, or to summarize the main idea of the letter in a brief, easy-to-read phrase.

In the follow-up letter, your P.S. should do two things. First, it should inform or entertain. You can use the P.S. to share interesting details about the apartments, inspirational quotes, or amusing bits of humor. Second, the P.S. should encourage the prospect to take further action. Ask them to schedule another visit for the purposes of leasing, or simply extend an invitation to your upcoming pool party. Whatever you do, end your letter with personality, and with a call to action. A well-written P.S. will help you do both.

No Matter What You Write . . .

Whether you send thank you cards, postcards, or letters, always make sure you *meticulously* proofread everything that goes out the door. If anything you send is marred by typographical errors or bad grammar, it will reflect poorly on you, your company, and/or your community. One more thing—hold off on the correcting fluid. "White out" is becoming less and less a part of today's word-processing culture, and as far as its use on professional correspondence is concerned, it is definitely a thing of the past. So be a perfectionist. Take the time to send your very best. Quite honestly, your prospects deserve nothing less.

TELEPHONE CALLS

In addition to written correspondence, telephone calling is an equally effective method for improving your chances with "be back" prospects. When making follow-up contacts by phone, keep the following principles in mind.

Determine where and when it's best to call. Most people appreciate being asked where and when it's most convenient for you to call. For example, if you've ever been phoned by a telemarketer at mealtime, you know that regardless of how fantastic their offer may be, their poor timing—combined with the unexpectedness of the call—greatly reduces their chances of success.

Some people prefer to be contacted at work. Others are forbidden to discuss personal matters on company time, and can only talk with you once they're off the clock. Some people don't get home from work until after 8:00 p.m. Still others are only available during certain times of the day, like mornings or late afternoons. Whatever the case, make sure that you determine where and when it's best to contact your prospects. It demonstrates your professionalism and ensures a more worth-while discussion once the connection is finally made.

Carefully organize your callbacks. When placing follow-up calls, it is possible to make more efficient use of your time by "bundling" your callbacks. As best you can, designate a certain portion of the day for making your follow-up calls. Or, if you have prospects who have given you permission to call them at home, place a number of your follow-up calls after regular business hours. This can be a very effective approach. Not only will it help free up additional time during your day, but it often results in a better overall conversation, since both parties are more relaxed and less distracted by the various demands of the workplace.

Another key benefit to organizing follow-up callbacks is that it enables you to establish a rhythm. You get your mind fully geared for the process, which helps you focus better. With every call you make, your objectives become clearer, your questions become more succinct, and your confidence steadily increases. Pretty soon, you're on a roll. You find "the zone," and that's when really good things start to happen.

Ask "am I catching you at a good time?" Let's say that you are my prospect, and I've called to invite you back for a second look. However, unbeknownst to me, you are just about to rush out the door when my call rings through. Being the considerate person you are, you answer anyway, even though you know it might not be such a good idea.

And how right you are. As soon as you answer, I launch into my spiel. On and on I go, oblivious to the fact that you were running late when I called, and that you're running even later now. At first, you listen patiently. But then, as precious minutes tick by, the tension begins to mount. Your patience turns to frustration. I keep on talking. The frustration turns to resentment. I still keep talking. Finally, with an attitude bordering on red-hot anger, you cut me off and—in so many words—tell me good-bye.

But that's not what you mean. In reality, what you're saying is *good riddance*.

Sound familiar? Haven't we all had experiences where inconsiderate callers have burned up our time when we didn't have time to spare? That is why, when placing follow-up calls, the first thing you should do is consider your prospect's circumstances at the moment your call goes through. If you are not sensitive to the issue of timing, you will run the risk of alienating your prospects and losing their business.

Therefore, in the very first moments of your conversation, you may want to ask your prospect this question: "Am I catching you at a good time?" They might say, "Sure." They might say, "I guess it's as good as any." Or they might say, "Actually, I'm right in the middle of a really big deadline. Can you call me back in an hour?"

Of the many secrets to success in placing follow-up calls, asking this question can really pay off. Not only does it demonstrate a rare level of respect for the person you are calling, but it also increases your odds of eventually having a fruitful conversation. If your caller is free, great—proceed with enthusiasm. If they are not, no problem; you can now reschedule the call for a time when they can more fully concentrate on what you have to say. So from now on, when making your calls, try opening with this question: "Am I catching you at a good time?" Doing so can significantly improve your chances of success.

Save the small talk. When you've placed the call and your prospect answers, especially if they're at work, it is generally best that you stick to business. Although it's possible, you probably aren't friends yet, which means there's not much basis for a social chat.

When a prospect indicates that your timing is good, *get to the point*. Most people don't want long-winded lead-ins or suspense. And in your greeting, try to avoid beginning with over-used questions like, "How's it goin'?" or "How are you today?" Not only are these largely superficial, but they sound amateurish. A much better alternative is to immediately explain the reason for your call. Be friendly and personable, of course, but keep your initial comments professional and focused. Concentrate first on addressing the business of helping them find their new apartment home. Then, if you sense that your prospect is willing and has the time, encourage conversation along more casual or personal lines.

What should you say? Obviously, the first thing you want to do in your follow-up contacts is determine whether or not the timing of your call is convenient. But what then? In much the same way you begin other conversations with your prospects, it is best to begin follow-up inquiries with a question. The more open-ended the question, the more quickly your conversation will develop. Avoid asking questions like, "Have you found an apartment yet?" Not only do questions of this nature generate yes or no responses—which as we've seen do very little to build a conversation—they also make you sound tacky, like you're trying to close a deal.

After establishing that it's a good time for your prospect to talk, make a brief transition and then get to the point. Here are just a few examples:

> *"I was thinking back to your visit the other day, and I was wondering:* ***What*** *have you decided on an apartment so far?"*
>
> *"I know you're busy, so I promise to keep this short.* ***How*** *is your apartment search coming along?"*
>
> *"We were just talking about how nice it would be to have you as our neighbor here at Heatherwood.* ***What*** *are your thoughts on the apartment we saw the other day?"*

Notice that these questions incorporate the open-ended words "what" and "how." They are designed to produce longer, more detailed responses from your prospects. Use the examples listed here, or better yet, create versions of your own. Just remember that you need to get your prospect talking before you can do anything else in the way of inviting them out for another look. You need to know what's on their mind. That means asking good, open-ended questions with a minimum of small talk, interjections, or explanation.

However, if you have a prospect you know is a very strong candidate, you can always be more direct. In fact, you may just want to come right out and ask, "When did you want to come back with your deposit?" Provided your prospect has arrived at a sufficient level of certainty, direct questions of this type are completely legitimate and extremely effective.

Center the conversation on your prospect. Again, the whole point of the follow-up call is to get your prospect to commit to a return visit. However, the only way they will is if you place clear emphasis on what is most important to them—their priorities, opinions, feelings, concerns, and so on. Unless the prospect feels that they're the center of your attention, their motivation to come back isn't likely to increase. Let them know that your top priority is to help them find the apartment that's right for them, and that you intend to do so without applying pressure. Finally, make sure your enthusiasm for serving their needs shines through. When you create a conversation that revolves around your prospect, you'll find that cooperation and commitment come much more easily.

If you must, leave a message. When the people you are trying to reach are unavailable, the next best thing is to leave them a message. If you choose to leave a message with a receptionist or on a prospect's answering device, here are some guidelines you can follow.

First, after specifying the date and time of your call, give your prospect a concrete reason to call you back. This is likely to require some advance thought and preparation. More than anything, you want to avoid saying that you're "just calling to see if they've found an apartment." If that's the only explanation you leave in your message, there's not much reason for them to return your call—especially if little or nothing has changed since you last spoke. Instead, give them something more concrete:

> *"Hi Pat, this is Chris Nolan with Olympic Heights Apartments. It's Thursday, October 12 at about 2 p.m. I'm calling for two reasons: First to let you know apartment F104 is still available; and second to see when might be a good time for you to come back out and have another look.*

Then, specify a time frame within which it would be best for them to return your call:

> *"I'll be in my office this afternoon between 2:30 and 4:00 p.m., and I can be reached at (323) 456-7890. Thanks a lot, Pat. I'll talk to you soon."*

Will people always call you back, during the time frame you've indicated? Not always, no. But using this approach will help increase your chances of a return call. Give people reasons to call you back, along with a range of times within which to do so. You'll be surprised at the difference a well-planned message can make.

Caution yourself against jumping to conclusions. Making follow-up calls can be frustrating, especially when you leave message after message for people who don't call you back. Sometimes, salespeople have a tendency to assume that people who aren't calling back are either being rude or evasive. While at times that may be true, you must caution yourself against jumping to that conclusion. Many times people have perfectly legitimate reasons for not returning your calls. Maybe they had to leave town unexpectedly on business. Perhaps they had trouble with their phone equipment, or got caught in a surprise traffic jam. Or, maybe they've been so busy with projects at work—or projects at home—that they haven't even had time to call their relatives, much less you.

No matter how rejected or insulted you may feel, understand that there might be a perfectly justifiable reason for your prospect's lack of communication. Then again, there might not.

In any case, give people the benefit of the doubt, and *remain loyal to them until they lease from you, or until they lease from someone else.*

THE COMBINATION METHOD

While written correspondence and telephone calling are effective in and of themselves, combining the two can produce even better and more reliable results.

Here's how the combination method works: Write a thank you card on the same day your prospect visits the community. Somewhere in the thank you card, again being careful not to sell, mention that you've marked your calendar to call them on a certain date and time. The note might read something like this:

> *Dear Chris,*
>
> *It was great to have you as our guest at Harbor Vista this afternoon. I really enjoyed seeing the pictures of your daughter, as well as hearing about your recent promotion. Congratulations!*
>
> ***I've marked my calendar to give you a call next Tuesday, at 5:45 p.m.*** *If you have any questions in the meantime, please let me know. I've enclosed my card for your convenience. Enjoy your weekend on the coast, and thanks again for visiting Harbor Vista.*
>
> *Sincerely,*

The most important thing for you to do is make certain that you schedule the follow-up call and place it as promised. As a fail-safe measure, schedule a reminder to yourself the day before. The combination approach is particularly effective, but it is entirely dependent on keeping your promise to call. If your call does not arrive on time, or if you don't call to reschedule if something comes up, your prospect's trust in you could be broken.

However, when your call *does* arrive on time, chances are much better that the prospect will be there to receive it. They'll have had reason to think about you periodically throughout their day, and might even have come up with some additional issues to discuss. Using the combination approach ultimately increases the likelihood that your prospect will be waiting for your call. The more you can improve the odds of actually making contact when you place the call, the better your chances for success will be.

A SIX-STEP FOLLOW-UP PLAN

The secret to maximizing results from your follow-up efforts is to have an organized plan. Having a plan helps you remain consistent, and consistency is vital to generating more leases through follow-up.

While you'll probably have to adjust for unique circumstances from time to time, here's a practical, flexible, and affordable plan you can use starting today:

- **Step One**—Make sure you obtain a completed guest card for each qualified prospect.
- **Step Two**—Create a filing system to keep the cards organized. A 4"× 6" card file box works best for storing guest cards on file (most guest cards are printed in a 4"× 6" format). Three different styles of "card guide" inserts are available:

  Alphabetical—for filing the cards by your prospects' last names

  Monthly—for filing the cards by projected move-in date or date of scheduled follow-up

  Plain—in the event you prefer a customized filing system. In most cases, you can purchase everything you need to create your system (file box and card guide inserts) for under 10 dollars. Creating a well-organized system will enable you to access and use the guest card information more efficiently. It will also minimize your chances of losing cards on days when you're buried in paperwork.
- **Step Three**—When your prospect leaves the office, sit down as immediately as you can and write a thank you card as outlined in the previous section (prompt action is very important, because the longer you wait, the fewer details you'll be able to remember about the time you spent together). Then, as we saw in the sample on pages 55 and 56, you might try indicating a time you'll check back with them by phone. Notice how this approach can help establish *consistency* in the process and further communicate your commitment to service.
- **Step Four**—Place the call as scheduled. This is the point where you want to begin "selling." Find out what your prospect has decided on an apartment so far. Then, in your own way, express to them that earning their business is important to you. If possible, present them with new and helpful information—in other words, "what's in it for them" if they lease. Prepare answers to any questions they may have had when last you spoke. And always be ready to suggest a time for another meeting. The objective is to increase their motivation and

enthusiasm to the level where they'll take action. When they commit to another visit, schedule a call to confirm, and remember to let them hang up first (see Secret 1).

- **Step Five**—Keep an eye out for things your future resident may find interesting, useful, or amusing. Examples might include articles on trends related to their line of work, flyers announcing discounts on mini-storage and child care services, or comics from the paper or a flip calendar. The idea is to stay in front of your prospect, and maintain a presence that says, "Hey—I'm interested in you as a person, and I'm still looking out for you." Remember, your goal is to build a *relationship* here. And even though you may not receive a reply (which isn't the point anyway), the extra effort can really give you a powerful advantage.
- **Step Six**—Continue with periodic telephone contacts (generally not more than once every two days) until your prospect reaches a decision. Be sensitive to their degree of readiness; if you feel it would be better to wait a few more days before contacting them again, wait. If you believe they're close to making a commitment, increase the frequency of your contacts and make something happen. No matter what, don't give up. *Stay with them until they decide to lease, or until they lease from someone else*. This is often what it takes to win the prospect's business. It is the very essence of going the extra mile.

PATIENCE IS A VIRTUE

We saw near the beginning of this secret that people's decisions to lease apartments can often require weeks, and even months, to reach. This means that sometimes we must be patient and wait. Leasing professionals who aren't willing to wait for prospects to decide won't enjoy the benefits of those decisions once they are made.

Though at times they may be frustrating, drawn-out leasing cycles often produce something far more valuable than quick solutions to vacancy problems. They produce loyal, trusting residents who appreciate your commitment to earning and keeping their business. Star leasing performance means putting your prospect's needs ahead of the desire for quick results, and in most cases doing that requires patience. Grant people the time they may need, and they'll be more likely to respond with the action you want.

WHEN ALL ELSE FAILS . . .

One of the hardest truths about a career in leasing is that we can never win 'em all. Eventually, all of us come face-to-face with the fact that some prospects were never meant to become our residents. When all else fails, and you simply cannot convince your prospect to leave a deposit, keep the following principles in mind.

Know when to move on. In the life of every leasing professional, there will come a time when you pour every ounce of your heart and energy into winning a prospect's business—and it simply does not come together. No matter how wonderful a person you are, how well you write, or how dynamic you are on the phone, someday a prospect is going to blow you off and never return. It's just an inevitable part of the apartment leasing landscape.

When you encounter people like this, believe in yourself enough to trust your instincts. If the person is clearly uncooperative and has no intentions of leasing, don't burn yourself out by beating your head against the wall. You don't need the aggravation. Conserve your energies for newer, more promising prospects. Give everyone the best and most thorough effort you possibly can. Then decide to move on.

Maintain your reputation. Even though someone may not lease from you, they may have a conversation with someone in the future that sounds something like this: "*You know, we never leased at Riverside Place, but the person who works there treated us better than anyone else we met.*" Always be mindful that the prospect who doesn't lease today might turn out to be a very valuable ally somewhere down the road.

Examine what didn't work—and learn from it. You read it in Secret 6: Part of knowing *what* to do is knowing what *not* to do. Taking those words of wisdom to heart can help you grow stronger as an apartment leasing professional. Every time you lose a prospect, whether it's to a competitor or something else, ask yourself: "What could I have done differently? How might I have changed the outcome?" Rather than hanging your head for not getting the business, look carefully for the reasons you

didn't get it. Chances are very good that you'll find small things that you can improve upon next time around. And if you can muster the courage, invite feedback from your prospect. Do the same from your supervisor and co-workers. Though it may take you well outside your comfort zone, make up your mind to learn from situations that do not work out.

Keep the door open. If it's clear that your prospect is not going to lease from you, ask them if it would be all right to keep in touch in the future. It's not uncommon for someone to leave your community, lease someplace else, then discover later that they should have listened to you in the first place. If in your final follow-up conversation you discover that your prospect did indeed lease someplace else, hope is definitely not lost. In most cases, the post office will forward mail to new addresses for a full year. This means in six or nine months you can mail to the address on the guest card and your prospect will still receive it.

S W S W S W N. If you've been searching for a way to cope with the rejection that follow-up sometimes brings about, I'll pass along to you what a friend passed along to me. S W S W S W N is a great "attitude adjuster" you can use when things aren't going your way. Here's what it stands for:

*Some **Will**. Some **Won't**. So **What**? **Next**!*

Whenever your follow-up efforts don't produce the desired results, just silently repeat these letters to yourself: **S W S W S W N**. If you've given a prospect everything you've got and they lease, great—**some will**. If you've given them all you've got and they don't, hey—**some won't**. And if after following up they still don't lease—**so what?** Bring on the **next** one, and remember: Failure doesn't happen when you fall down. Failure happens when you *stay* down. Get back up, and keep on trying. That's how champions are made.

REVIEW

Follow-up is the process by which we continue contacting prospects who have not yet leased in an ongoing attempt to earn their business. There are five important reasons for maintaining a consistent follow-up program.

1. Helps generate higher returns on advertising investments
2. Effectively neutralizes prospect procrastination
3. Increases awareness of your apartments—and you
4. Reveals additional objections
5. Gives those who do it consistently a tremendous competitive edge.

There are three essential rules of follow-up:

Rule number one: Obtain guest card information from qualified prospects
Rule number two: Communicate specifically in terms of your prospect
Rule number three: Ask for a commitment.

Popular methods of follow-up include

Written correspondence
Telephone calls
Combining the two for maximum effect.

Starting today, you can begin using a six-step plan for effective follow-up:

1. Obtain completed guest cards from qualified prospects
2. Create an efficient filing system
3. Write a thank you card
4. Follow the card with a telephone call
5. Follow the telephone call with a letter
6. Continue with telephone contacts until your prospect decides to lease from you, or until they lease from someone else.

In your follow-up efforts, when all else fails

Know when to move on
Maintain your reputation
Examine what didn't work—and learn from it
Keep the door open to future opportunities
Remember: **S**ome **W**ill. **S**ome **W**on't. **S**o **W**hat? **N**ext!

Finally, failure doesn't happen when you fall down. Failure happens when you *stay* down.

Profile of a Superstar

Beginning in the spring of 1994, graduates of my *Performance Leasing* seminar were each asked to complete a survey that examined their style of selling. The results were remarkable; data gathered from the seminars consistently indicated that there were certain traits shared in common by exceptional performers in the business. Then, as *The 7 Secrets to Successful Apartment Leasing* was nearing completion during the fall of 1995, it became clear that such information would be a valuable addition to the book. Therefore, a special project was launched: To build a "performance profile" of an apartment leasing superstar.

The profile was created using state-of-the-art performance assessment software obtained from a Seattle-based employee research company. After carefully considering the various evaluation instruments that were available, two specialized surveys were selected—one measuring personal values and another measuring behavioral styles.

At this point, it is important to explain the reasoning behind why these particular instruments were chosen. For years, experts in the field of psychology have recognized that a person's overall "success pattern" can be seen in a measurable combination of the following variables:

Values	40%
Behavior	30%
Intellect	10%
Education/Experience	10%
Training	10%
Total	**100%**

As you can see, this theory suggests that the overwhelming majority of a person's potential for success is based upon the nature of their core values, and the behavior which comes as a result. Therefore, it became evident that the most reliable way to discover the true secrets of apartment leasing superstars would be to evaluate them on the basis of their *values* and their *behavior*.

Once the survey tools had been selected, the next and most critical step was finding the best possible candidates for the study. Companies representing every facet of the multi-family housing industry, from REITs and national property management companies to owner/operators and smaller firms, were contacted and asked which of their leasing professionals they felt would best qualify. After numerous individuals were nominated and considered, 10 finalists were selected—all top-caliber leasing experts with certifiable credentials. Included among them were people who had received such prestigious honors as Employee of the Year, Top Leasing Consultant, Best On-Site Manager for 1995, and 1995 Rookie of the Year. (It was agreed, in the interests of both the finalists and their employers, that all names would be held in strict confidence.)

Once the test group had been selected, each finalist was asked to complete the two surveys. The first measured their *Personal Values and Interests*—**why** they do what they do (values). The second evaluated their *Selling Styles*—**how** they achieve the results they achieve (behavior). Once the responses were gathered from each finalist, the results were reviewed by a trained research expert and then summarized for publication.

What you are about to read is a fascinating glimpse into the high-performance world of apartment leasing superstars. While the information is undeniably beneficial, it is important to note that there were many varia-

tions among the participants' scores, which suggests that performance profiling of this nature is not an exact science.

PERSONAL VALUES AND INTERESTS SURVEY

Apartment leasing superstars (hereafter referred to as "stars") appear to demonstrate a highly consistent pattern of key values that underlie and influence their performance. Following are a number of the star values revealed by this research:

- Stars seek new knowledge primarily to gain results. They are practical and more intuitive in their approach to acquiring knowledge, preferring to *apply* it rather than *accumulate* it. As best they can, they absorb information on a "need to know" basis; it helps them manage their time and energies more effectively.
- Stars are not typically driven by the need to acquire great sums of money. While compensation is clearly important, stars tend to place greater emphasis on balancing their efforts to make money with other important areas in their lives. To the star, financial reward is more a product of adhering to their values and beliefs than it is the result of "drive" or raw ambition.
- Stressful and unpleasant surroundings do not seriously depress this person or stifle their creativity.
- Stars are genuinely concerned about the welfare of others. There is a tendency for them to want to give everyone an opportunity to succeed, especially those they believe are hard-working and sincere. "Fairness" is very important to stars, because they believe that everyone deserves equal opportunity. This value drives the star to make decisions that will help the greatest number of people in the greatest number of ways.
- Power and control are not primary motivators. Stars are typically more patient and less ego-driven than the norm, which helps explain their unique talent for establishing positive relationships. A team player, the star will often tackle daily challenges not for their own benefit, but for the benefit of their customers and co-workers

alike. Stars are also exceptional at leading others, preferring a low-pressure and consultative approach. They may even allow others to set the pace, as long as it will produce the results they desire in the end.

- Stars function well in environments governed by clear guidelines and structure. When their responsibilities are well-defined, star performers rarely require close supervision.
- Trustworthiness and integrity are hallmarks of the superstar, as are loyalty and the desire to represent their companies with pride.

As mentioned previously, *values* are the dominant factors that influence a person's behavior. And behavior, in turn, is what ultimately shapes a person's performance. For example, the stressful—and sometimes confrontational—leasing office environment does not depress leasing superstars, nor does it seem to stifle their creativity. This means that prospects walking through the door are rarely met with impatience or negative attitudes. Rather, in most cases superstars are able to insulate their prospects from leasing office tension, greet them with warmth, and proceed with a dynamic presentation. This is one type of exemplary behavior that strong foundational values can produce.

We can all benefit from taking a closer look at the values which drive our levels of performance. Ask yourself, "Which of the values listed here are consistent with my outlook on apartment leasing? Which are different? And what changes might I make to bring my performance more into line with that of the stars in our industry?"

SELLING STYLES ANALYSIS

In 1928, noted psychologist Dr. William Marston developed a system that he used to describe key aspects of people's behavior. Known as the DISC model, it measures four different behavioral characteristics that exist, to some degree or another, in each of us.

D Dominance—how we respond to problems or challenges
I Influence—how we influence others to our point of view

S Steadiness—how we respond to the pace of our environments

C Compliance—how we respond to rules and procedures

Over time, the DISC model has been adapted to help evaluate behavioral styles in various groups of people—including sales professionals. One of the DISC adaptations is known as the Selling Styles Analysis (SSA), which was created to identify areas of strength and weakness in people who sell for a living. Since apartment leasing professionals obviously fit this description, each of the ten top performers in the study group was asked to complete the SSA.

Again, while numerous variations were observed from individual to individual, a uniform "style profile" gradually emerged. Most interesting was the fact that *every star in the group* scored strongly in the I category, indicating that each of them possesses a strong desire and ability to influence others. Apartment leasing superstars exhibiting "High I" behavior are identified by a distinctive range of characteristics.

Words to describe—charming, confident, convincing, enthusiastic, inspiring, persuasive, popular, sociable, and trusting. *The superstar's predominant emotion is* ***optimism.***

Ideal work environment—one which provides a high degree of people contact, freedom from control and detail, freedom of movement, a forum for ideas to be heard, and democratic supervision.

Value to the company—the "High I" is optimistic and enthusiastic, creative in problem solving, instrumental in motivating others toward their goals, and able to negotiate conflicts with poise and self-confidence.

Tendencies under stress—self-promoting, overly talkative, unrealistic, too optimistic.

Possible limitations—inattentive to details, unrealistic in appraising prospects, trusting people without sufficient grounds, and situational or inconsistent listening.

There were also a number of other common threads—strengths and weaknesses alike—that became clear in the SSA reports. In no particular order, they include:

- Positive sense of humor
- Uses emotion and animation in presentations
- People oriented
- Welcomes objections/addresses them up-front
- Strong listening skills
- Direct, positive, and friendly when closing
- Dislikes detail work
- Negotiates conflict—turns confrontations into positives
- Resists cold calls
- Handles high numbers of activities/customers at once
- Paints vivid word pictures
- Motivates and builds confidence in others

The Selling Styles Analysis is a remarkable assessment tool: It produces objective and extremely accurate information about how salespeople perform on the job. It illuminates one's greatest strengths, providing a tremendous boost of reinforcement to the things they do well. It also helps identify areas that are in need of further improvement. And, the SSA is ideal for use in conjunction with traditional shopping reports. Unlike typical shopping reports, which show how a person performed during one particular effort on one particular day, the SSA defines what people are most likely to do on *any* given day—clearly a much broader (and potentially more useful) perspective to draw.

In short, both the Personal Values and Interests Survey and the SSA hold great value as personal development and training tools for apartment leasing professionals.

SUMMARY

Without question, there are many characteristics and many different environmental variables that can influence a person's performance in the leasing office. Nevertheless, the information revealed by this research points to an important conclusion: Personal values, and the behaviors which result, are the foundations for success in apartment leasing. Even though intelligence, education, experience, and training are important, they cannot begin to take the place of a person's true character.

There is, however, a flipside to the research viewpoint. That is the practical perspective of reality. As essential as they are, sound values and exceptional behavior have never been the exclusive guarantors of success. There are other real-life virtues that round out the personal success equation: compassion, courage, determination, faith, humility, love, persistence, personal responsibility, purpose, self-discipline, servitude, and vision, among others. Without these in our possession, it may be virtually impossible for us to experience the joy of reaching our full potential.

Final Thoughts

I'm going to leave you with seven principles I've had the good fortune to discover thus far in my exciting and educational journey through life.

1. If experiencing life to the fullest is the dream we pursue, we must stay motivated. People who fail to keep themselves motivated on a regular basis are sitting ducks for self-doubt, worry, and stress. It has been said that staying motivated is a lot like eating. If we feed ourselves balanced, healthy meals each day, our bodies and minds remain strong. However, if we go too long without food, or eat things that are not good for us, we grow lethargic and weak. The same goes for motivation. If we surround ourselves with inspiring ideas and uplifting people, we continually increase our levels of performance. If we do not, we become stagnant and ineffective. Worse, we become vulnerable to the negative tendencies of our nature. Make the commitment to spend time each day with positive information and positive people. Stay motivated. Stay strong.
2. Living a day without goals is like climbing aboard an airplane without knowing its final destination. Once airborne, we know we're moving forward, but we have no idea how far we'll be going, how long the trip will take, or where we'll eventually wind up. Sure, we

could just sit back, go along for the ride, and wait for whatever blind luck decides to send our way. But like the imaginary plane ride, merely waiting for luck in life involves a tremendous amount of uncertainty. By setting specific goals however, we can eliminate much of that uncertainty. We can increase the probability of actually achieving the things we most desire. And we can more successfully adapt to change, which in a sense is the only constant we can depend on. So start planning. Start writing your goals today. No matter what you do, for as long as you live, your life will be subject to change. You can either be the master of that change, or you can be a victim of it.

3. People not doing anything with their lives will try to discourage you from doing anything with yours. Don't let them succeed. Take a stand against the naysayers of the world. Refuse to accept mediocrity. And even if you fail in the pursuit of something you thought at first would be successful, always remember these ageless words from the great Theodore Roosevelt:

"The credit belongs to the man who is actually in the arena; whose face is marred by dust and sweat and blood; who strives valiantly; who errs and comes short again and again; who knows the great enthusiasms, the great devotions, and spends himself in a worthy cause; who at the best knows the triumph of high achievement; and who, at the worst, if he fails at least fails while daring greatly, so that his place shall never be with those cold and timid souls who know neither victory nor defeat."

4. Always give more than what it takes. Greatness has never been achieved merely by meeting the minimum requirements, and exceptional effort is the surest way to achieve exceptional rewards. Make it your personal challenge, starting today, to do a little more than what is expected in everything you do. Not only will the fruits of your labor increase, but you'll steadily acquire the habit of going the extra mile (which is the one place in life you'll never find a crowd).

5. Positive energy produces positive results, in the same way that negative energy produces negative results. When we smile and reach out to the world, it almost always reaches back. When we frown and pull away, the world almost always does the same. Every day we have an important choice to make. We can either enter the day projecting positive energy, or we can enter the day projecting negative energy. Projecting negative energy is easy; there are always plenty of reasons to be mad, sad, or afraid. But projecting positive energy is tougher; it means sometimes going against the grain of the world in which we live. Remind yourself each day that being positive, no matter what the circumstance, builds perseverance. Perseverance builds character. Character, in turn, builds hope. And hope is what keeps our dreams alive.
6. The responsibility for making our way in life is ours and ours alone. In the final analysis, when we study great leaders in our history we see a common thread throughout their characters: the courage to take responsibility for their actions. However, people of sound mind and body who shirk responsibility for the things they do exert enormous burdens on society. They make excuses. They shift the blame. And in so doing, they demonstrate an outright disrespect for the freedoms and opportunities that have been protected and made available to us all. If we are to achieve meaningful success in our lives—be it financial, in relationships, or otherwise—we must recognize our obligation to accept full responsibility for our actions. When we do, those same great threads of character will show forth in us as well.
7. No matter what career path we ultimately choose in life, every penny of every paycheck we earn comes from someone else. In professional apartment leasing that someone, of course, is the resident. The better we are at winning their business, the more certain we can be of receiving our just reward. However, the process of winning new residents (as this book was written to address) represents only one side of the equation. Keeping them, of course, represents the other.

Conclusion

In closing, I want to acknowledge the fact that apartment leasing can be a tough business. Often we work in isolation, which can cause us to feel lonely and vulnerable. It can be hard to effectively manage our time, because we never know when the phone will ring or when future residents will walk in. It can be utterly disheartening when, after reaching 98 percent occupancy, the owners decide to raise our rents and 30 more people decide to move out. Back to the old drawing board.

Those are some of the more challenging realities. But just as there are difficulties, there are also tremendous rewards to be gained in the work we do. Where else can you establish—and maintain—such a high number of long-term, gratifying customer relationships than in the multihousing industry? Where else can you impact people's daily lives in such a positive and tangible way as we do? And where else can you so quickly earn the right to basically run your own multi-million dollar small business?

All things considered, we are fortunate indeed. Thank you for taking the time to read this book. I hope you've found it helpful. May God richly bless your efforts as you invest your time and energies in the service of others.

Index

Index

Note: Boldface numbers indicate illustrations.

Index

About the Author

Eric Cumley spent over 10 years marketing and managing apartments, conducting leasing seminars, and designing apartment advertising campaigns with For Rent magazine. He currently works as a Certified Financial Planner®.

www.ingramcontent.com/pod-product-compliance
Lightning Source LLC
Chambersburg PA
CBHW060337100426
42812CB00003B/1032